£14.95

THE ROLE OF LOCAL GOVERNMENT IN EDUCATION:

Assuring quality and accountability

Stewart Ranson
Centre for Education Management and
Policy Studies

Longman Industry and Public Service Management,
Longman Group UK Limited,
The High, Harlow, Essex, CM20 1YR, England
and Associated Companies Throughout the World.
Telephone Harlow (0279) 442601; Fax Harlow (0279) 444501;
Telex 81491 Padlog

First published 1992

A catalogue record for this book is available from the British Library

ISBN 0-582-09244-2

Typeset by Midland Book Typesetters Ltd
Printed by Bell and Bain Ltd., Glasgow

Contents

Part 1

1
The LEA in question

Is the local education authority really necessary? And if it is what should be the appropriate role of the LEA? These interesting questions are, arguably, the most important facing education at the present time, more significant than all the controversy surrounding testing or the national curriculum. For the questions raised involve issues about the nature of our democracy, what constitutes effective management of institutions and what are the preconditions for achievement of young people in classrooms. Whether the LEA makes any difference is, therefore, not only the hottest political question of the moment it is also the most intriguing intellectual question – does the LEA matter to the quality of learning for a child at school? (This is of course to pose the question, for the time being, in terms of the limits of the current debate, setting aside whether the LEA is important for adult retraining, vocational preparation and the regeneration of depressed local economies, or the abstract purposes of a learning society.)

The LEA for much of the post war period was the centre-piece in a complex partnership of educational interests incorporating Whitehall, town and county hall, schools, colleges and their clients. The LEA was responsible for many of the considerable achievements of the post-war period: managing the post-war redevelopment of the service including the massive building programme and recruitment of teachers to respond to the birth bulge, the pioneering development of comprehensive schools, of new examinations (the GCSE) and of assessing achievement (records of achievement).

By the 1980s, however, the LEAs had become the focus of critical analysis from particular groups in society. The pamphleteers of the Conservative New Right[1], for example, the Adam Smith Institute, and the Institute of Economic Affairs, and the Hillgate Group have argued that educational standards have been in decline and much of the blame lies with the LEAs who have encouraged poor management, remote bureaucracy, denied public choice and prevented due accountability to parents and employers. The LEA, it is proposed, is no longer required, because schools can fulfil its traditional functions, or if it is, only in a limited vestigial form.

Nevertheless, in the ensuing 1988 Education Reform Act, the Conservative Government's response to such New Right analysis, the LEA survived. Indeed, although its powers were considerably reduced its strategic responsibilities were, it was proclaimed, increased. Quality and accountability now depended upon the strategic role of the LEA in monitoring standards and enabling schools to implement the National Curriculum effectively.

Yet, hardly two years since passing the most radical reworking of the government of education since the 1944 Education Act questions are being asked once more about the rationale and role of the LEA as well as issues of expenditure control.

Mr Heseltine, Secretary of State for the Environment, announced in February 1991 that his Review of Local Government would have education at the top of his agenda: options being widely conjectured at the time were the transfer of teachers' salaries, or the costs of further education colleges, or, indeed the wholesale transfer of education from local to central government.

The Times, of 20 February 1991, reported that Mr Clarke, Secretary of State for Education and Science, 'backs changes in education funding' yet *Education* in the same week said that Mr Clarke was 'fighting a rearguard action to keep education spending under local government control'. This seemed the more accurate account and Mr Clarke won a battle within cabinet to prevent education being transferred to central government; acknowledging that it would not provide the quick fix for the poll tax which Mr Heseltine purportedly was striving for.

What Mr Clarke has been promoting instead, however, is the idea that all schools should opt out of local authority control: 'Conservatives seek opt-out for all schools within five years' (*Guardian* 4 March 1991). In January the Conservatives' Education Advisory Group reported that it was aiming to ensure that there was hardly a school left under local authority control (*Guardian* 4 January 1991).

In a radio interview on *The World this Weekend* (23 March 1991) Mr Clarke set out, more systematically, his view of the future government of education. He believed that the natural progression for schools was to move from the local management of schools (LMS) to grant maintained school status (GMS). The only issue for him was the pace of this change and the Government might be willing to introduce amending legislation to ensure that

GM schools became the normality. Legislation would certainly be introduced in the near future, he confirmed, to enable all further education, tertiary and sixth form colleges to become autonomous from the LEA. Then RIP LEA? LEAs in future would have no routine management role in schools or colleges. They would, rather, become 'enabling' authorities, a smaller role but very important in relation to special education, music, truancy and difficult to place pupils – 'an LEA is needed to do this'. This is a service role for the LEA. The question for Mr Clarke, therefore, was not whether there should be an LEA, but whether it needed powers to fulfil the roles which are inescapable to it.

The *Independent* on Sunday 24 March 1991, however, reported that ministers had conceded that if local authorities lost control of education in any future reorganisation, or large numbers of schools opted out, then the Government would have, nevertheless, to create a new tier of administration. Mr Clarke, it was suggested, was considering the introduction of government appointed regional committees (similar to the regional health authorities) which would coordinate services such as special needs, the inspectors, allocate resources and review staffing levels. This idea of regional boards was taken up and highlighted in a paper put forward by leading Conservatives on the political committee of the Carlton Club who wanted LEAs to be replaced by regional boards (*Guardian* 29 April 1991). The boards would act as buffers between individual schools and central government, as well as monitoring standards and overseeing education for children with special needs. This paper had been put forward as the Conservatives begin to consider how to manage large numbers of opted out schools.

The Prime Minister, Mr Major, no less than his two predecessors, began to take a leading role in the development of the education service. In May, he launched the White Paper on Education and Training which, amongst other things, hives off all further, tertiary and sixth form colleges from local authority control in 1993 to be financed by new funding councils. And on 4 July, in a major speech to the right wing Centre for Policy Studies, the Prime Minister argued for the need to break up 'the monolith' of the local education system. He announced that there would be legal changes to allow cheaper forms of city technology colleges and that the Government's commitment to encouraging opting out would be enhanced: Local authorities would have limits set on their campaigning against school proposals to attain GM status. The Prime Minister confessed that the Government had been providing incentives to encourage schools to opt out of local authority control. His Citizens' Charter launched in July will further weaken the influence of LEAs over local education: there is to be more delegation – of inspection and possibly education welfare – more opting out and contracting out, while there is to be increased lay involvement in admission appeals and in the inspection of schools.

A *Sunday Times* leader (28 July 1991) exhorts the Prime Minister to brook no delay in implementing the policy of opting out which it believes is the solution to the problems facing education but is being obstructed by local councils:

> Opting out is the centrepiece of the Government's education reforms, an attempt to reinvigorate our state system with standards, discipline and pride by allowing schools to break free from the dead hand of local authority control and sink or swim on the basis of the pupils they can attract which, in turn, will depend on the quality of the education they offer. Schools that establish a good reputation will prosper, for parents will queue up to send their children to them and with each child will come more government money. Those that fail to attract enough pupils will be allowed to go bust. That is a better way of deciding which schools should be closed and which expanded than the bureaucratic fiat of those who run education in places like Newham. Above all it offers the opportunity, for the first time since the grammar schools were abolished, in an act of official vandalism unmatched since Henry VIII ransacked the monasteries, of replacing the culture of mediocrity which now permeates the state system with a climate for competition which encourages competition in state schooling.

By July 1991, however, ministers were concluding that, for the time being, LEAs might survive their review of the future government of education. Conservative think tank proposals to devolve education to district councils or to set up a new regional tier of administration would now probably not be taken up, because county councils were believed to be better placed to deliver strategic planning of school provision and special education. Yet Mr Eggar, the Education Minister, told the annual conference of the Council of Local Education Authorities (CLEA) that LEAs would survive but only 'on probation' for the future running of schools. He attacked some local authorities for their obstructiveness in their campaigns to prevent schools opting out: engaging in petty obstruction of the kind which brings local authorities into disrepute. Such doctrinaire attitudes are 'an anachronism':

> Local government does not have a natural monopoly of responsibility for planning the future pattern of schools and colleges; nor does it have a natural monopoly in arrangements for inspection and quality assurance . . . That philosophy belongs to a different era, it should now be put aside . . . (the LEA) places too much emphasis on the system and not enough on individual schools.

As might be expected, the attitudes Ministers have displayed throughout the year towards local education authorities, have not been well received even by Conservative run Councils. In May, in an interview with the *Times Educational Supplement (TES)*, Mr Macnamara, the leader of Hampshire County Council denounced the plan to remove colleges from local authority control and the general denigration of local government by Ministers: the Secretary of State seemed 'hell-bent on destroying local education authorities without any idea of what to put in their place' (*TES* 17 May 1991). The Chief Executive of Devon County Council has commented that LEAs had an enduring role not least to rescue failed policies and educational mistakes. 'The case was recently proved with alarm over reading standards and LEAs now looked like being called in to rescue the National Curriculum – a role which even (the minister) had the grace to recognise' (*Education* 26 July 1991).

The Association of Metropolitan Authorities (AMA) is clear about the implications of recent Government policy initiatives for the future of the local education authority. The first edition of *Review of Local Government*, is entitled 'LEAs face threat of withering on the vine':

> It appears to be the Government's intention to let LEAs 'wither on the vine.
>
> The Education Reform Act began the process by allowing all secondary schools and larger primary schools to opt out of LEAs. Now all primary schools can do so as well. The Act also removed polytechnics from LEAs. Now the Government plans to remove further education colleges, tertiary colleges and sixth form colleges – handing them over to quangos – and Training and Enterprise Councils are to become involved in the Careers Service.
>
> (AMA Summer 1991)

The *Review* contends that there are many reasons why 'the Government's attack on LEAs' should be resisted: 'there are sound financial and adminstrative reasons . . . but above all we need LEAs because they are democratically accountable'.

The *Times* in a leader article (23 March 1991) also expressed concern at 'the drift to the centre'. While acknowledging the sensible delegation of responsibilities under local management of schools and colleges which have made LEAs less bureaucratic the article counsels against the dismantling of one of the pillars of local government – local education:

> Local government may stand the loss of the colleges, and may even learn to treat those institutions that remain to it with greater sensitivity than in the past. But at a certain point the pass will have been sold. A community's schools are the quintessential local institutions, symbols of

communal strength and concord. They are locally financed, governed and administered in democracies around the world. To conclude that this cannot be achieved in Britain – simply because it has not worked well where the London elite happens to live – is an admission of collective constitutional defeat. Add the schools to the colleges in Mr Clarke's burgeoning empire and it will be hardly worth Mr Heseltine's time reforming local democracy. It will have nothing to do.

Yet, it is not only 'right wing' groups and the Conservative Government which seem committed to the radical diminution or demise of the LEA. In June the *Independent* published a 'Schools Charter: A Policy Study for Education in the Nineties'. It argues that the Government's policy of piecemeal opting out is disastrously confused and can only 'lead to increasing chaos, with local education authorities battling to retain control over their local school systems, while some groups of parents and governors grow disillusioned and disaffected'. It advocates the disappearance of local authority control of schools:

> The role which local councils play in running schools needs to be cleanly and simply abolished, as soon as schools are ready . . . Once the break is made between local councils and schools, the funding of schools should be greatly simplified. It would appear to voters who was responsible for underfunding: the government . . .
>
> The sole objection is that the administration of schools would be 'centralised' and that schools would lose their 'local' quality . . . But it does not stand up to scrutiny.
>
> Matters which should properly be national policy – the broad curriculum framework, regulation of standards, and the amount of taxpayers' money spent on schools – would indeed be decided centrally. But schools themselves would be *more* local than they are now. They would be answerable to, and indeed managed by, their immediate communities, in the most complete way possible.
>
> (p.24–25).

The function of LEAs would, in this scheme of things, be to provide an advisory and inspection service, as part of a national standards authority, and to provide services to schools on a contractual basis should they wish to purchase them. Residual roles – such as the careers service (and special needs?) would remain with local councils.

Other experts (as reported in *Education* 26 July 1991) have been portending the necessary demise of the LEA: 'Sir Christopher Ball, the guru of post-school education, believed the advent of the single market had made the LEAs obsolete and that education planning and coordination now had to take place at regional level. His colleague Mr David Bradshaw told the CLEA conference politely that it was time they retired gracefully from the field. Dr Keith Hampson MP, Mr Heseltine's 'brains' at the Department of the Environment, thought that education had been with local government for 90 years and that was about long enough. He was clearly meditating a different future in which funding went directly to institutions from central government or else to school boards'.

A debate about the future of local government in education is apparently thriving. The Government has, it seems, determined for the time being at least to retain the LEA in the scheme of local education management yet is clearly committed to a programme of 'deregulating' LEA control. The trend for the future government of education seems clear: an acceleration towards greater delegation of responsibility to schools, with most opting out of LEA control over the next three to five years. The LEA would then either disappear or become, as it is even now being encouraged to, no more than a service agency which would survive only if schools chose to use it. This would be a very different conception of the role of the LEA in local education from that implied in the 1988 Education Reform Act which accorded to local government the strategic tasks of planning and quality assurance. Now even this contribution is being diminished. Yet whereas the 1988 constitutional reforms were subject to the legislative procedures of Parliament, these transitions, arguably of greater constitutional import because of their significance for the status of local government in education, are being carried through by edict and regulation.

This book is based upon a larger programme of research, supported by the Economic and Social Research Council, into the changing governance and management of education following the 1988 Education Reform Act. That study seeks to identify the different kinds of local system of education that are emerging across the country. This book focuses more specifically upon the new roles of the local education authority and has grown out of a report sponsored by the Local Government Management Board to identify the different perspectives on the management of education as illustrated in the implementation of the Education Reform Act.

How LEAs would respond to the management challenge presented by the ERA reforms was by no means straightforward. Despite the uniform prescriptions there was scope for considerable variety of interpretation in how the legislation should be managed locally. The study sought to identify a small number of LEAs each of which formed a distinctive perspective upon the Education Reform Act and how it should be interpreted and implemented. These LEAs are not presented here because their services are in some way exemplary: they would not presume this to be the case, each having their own problems and making mistakes as well as realising aspirations. Their value is the distinctive vision and leadership they have brought to the management of their service and the potential this reveals for alternative interpretation and choice about future development.

In each of the four chosen case studies – Enfield, Kent, Manchester and Warwickshire – the discussion will review their approach to setting up the new management: which values and purposes have been chosen to inform the management of change, their conception of the new roles and relationships of the LEA, and their perspective upon learning quality, local management of schools, performance and accountability.

The case studies then focus upon how LEAs have faced up, over the last twelve to eighteen months, to expenditure cuts, opting out and the proposals contained in the White Paper on Education and Training. The discussion in the case studies is presented largely in their own words (either from reports or interview notes) to capture the distinctiveness of their language and perspective. Interviews in the LEAs were conducted in every case with the chief education officer, the chief adviser or inspector, and the senior officer responsible for developing the formula and implementing the local management of schools. Other interviews have been conducted with a chair of education, and senior officers responsible for post 16 education, and the management of area offices. In this book I have chosen to give considerable space to the distinctive and articulate voices of the chief education officers.

In Chapters 3 to 6 there will be a discussion of what is special about the approach of each LEA as well as what they have in common in the new management of education. This is followed by a concluding discussion of those roles and tasks which are, I believe, inescapably dependent upon the contribution of local government if effective education is to be achieved.

I am grateful to a number of people who have provided support in the preparation of this study. In particular of course I am grateful to the chief education officers and their colleagues who generously gave me time and documentary materials to improve my understanding of what they have been trying to achieve. They deserve much better. Dr Bob Morris, education officer of the AMA has been very helpful. I am grateful to colleagues who have offered critical analysis within the research programme: Alison Bullock, Peter Ribbins, Kathryn Riley, John Stewart, Hywel Thomas and Kieron Walsh. I would like to thank the Economic and Social Research Council for their sponsorship of the main programme of research and Steve Voyce, who as leader of the Education Project at the Local Government Training Board commissioned the specific report on LEA management, for his encouragement during the study. Roger Henwood of Longmans and Mark Sheldrake of the Local Government Management Board have provided helpful advice and been patient. Jenny Neave's secretarial skills have been indispensable. And without Helena's good will in sharing her holiday with papers, books and word processors this book would not have been completed. I am of course responsible for the evident flaws that, in spite of all this support, remain.

Notes

[1] *The Omega File on Education*, Adam Smith Institute, 1984; *Whose Schools? A Radical Manifesto*, The Hillgate Group, 1986; S. Sexton, *Our Schools – A Radical Policy*, Institute of Economic Affairs, 1987.

2
The restructuring of local education

The reform of education and, in particular, the local government of education has been at the centre of the Conservative Government's priorities. The 1988 Education Reform Act created the most radical recasting of the government of education since 1944. The Act redefined the relationships between central and local government so as to strengthen Whitehall's control over the curriculum, diminished the administrative powers LEAs have over their institutions, and sought to make schools and colleges more responsive to the wishes of parents and employers. Through these changes the Act created what has been called 'an administered market'. The intention of the legislation, however, was not only to redefine roles and responsibilities of the education partners but to do so as part of a broader reconstituting of the government of education according to new values of public choice and accountability. If government could become responsive and accountable to the public conceived as consumers then educational standards, it was proposed, would improve.

For the Government, the 1988 reforms had their origins in a number of concerns which had grown over time and increasingly coalesced in demands for a change in the system as a whole. Standards of achievement it was claimed were in decline, and this was affecting the economic health and well-being of the nation. Moreover, there was a need to ensure more efficient use of public expenditure in education and value for money in the service's scarce resources.

Local education authorities received much of the blame for the purported problems of poor educational standards. Where they were not charged with directly promoting policies – for example, anti racism, sex education, peace studies – which the Government regarded as anathema they were said to be locked into a culture of detailed administration which stifled schools and prevented them from managing their affairs effectively. LEAs needed to delegate the detail while focusing on matters of strategy and quality which were appropriate to their role. LEAs were to have their powers reduced but their role remained strategically important. A new system of local management emerged with local government offered, albeit on trial, a significant status within it. Yet hardly has the ink dried on the new legislative settlement and, with most local authorities embracing their new role with some enthusiasm, the debate about their rationale has begun again in earnest.

Since the autumn of 1990, the existence and role of the LEA has once more been the focus of critical scrutiny and there appears to be a new thrust to nationalise education. There have been four principal components to this new development: the first has been the Government's scramble to find ways of reducing the community charge, or poll tax, one option in which has been to consider removing parts or the whole of education; the second has been the White Paper on Education and Training, which proposes to remove further education, tertiary and sixth form colleges from LEA control. It seems reasonable to assume that at least part of the motive for this initiative lies in reducing the poll tax, yet it is unlikely that this is the whole explanation, the understanding of which will involve a grasp of the Government's strategy for post compulsory education; the third and, perhaps most significant reason lies in the Government's wish to reinvigorate their policy of allowing schools to opt out of local authority control as part of an ostensible strategy of weakening the LEA and diminishing its role. The fourth and latest change is outlined in the Schools Bill which removes the LEA's control over the inspection of their schools. This chapter will discuss the incipient trend towards the nationalisation of education implied by these recent initiatives together with their origins in the Education Reform Act.

The 1988 Education Reform Act

One of the leading administrators of the legislation set out clearly the objectives of the Education Reform Act in a public lecture (Stuart 1989):

(i) above all, *to raise standards of attainment for all pupils* by a better definition of what is to be taught and learnt; the greater involvement of a better informed parent body; and greater autonomy and hence responsibility for individual schools in the way in which they deploy all their resources to this end;
(ii) what is thus involved is to increase substantially public information available to parents about what pupils are to be taught; what they have achieved; what the resources of the school are; and how the school

deploys them. *Better accountability applied to more informed parental choice,* which various aspects of the Act seek to enlarge;
(iii) to improve the overall management of the service by delegating decision-making as close as possible to the point where the decisions bite. *Better Management* and a better curriculum go hand in hand.

The Education Reform Act strives to realise these objectives with two principal strategies: firstly, by establishing more rigorous planning of teaching and learning throughout the system. The creation of a National Curriculum would provide an entitlement to broad and balanced learning for all five to sixteen year olds while achievement would be assessed by a range of assessment procedures. Such close monitoring of progress in learning would enable parents to know more clearly what was being studied, what objectives were being set and what was being achieved individually and collectively. This kind of information would provide the basis of the second principal strategy of increasing the accountability of the service to parents and the public generally. Introducing the Bill in Parliament, the Secretary of State said:

> The Bill will galvanise parental involvement in schools. Parents will have more choice. They will have greater variety of schools to choose from. We will create new types of schools. Parents will be far better placed to know what their children are being taught and what they are learning ... And the Bill will introduce competition into the public provision of education. This competition will introduce a new dynamic into our schools system which will stimulate better standards all round.

(DES 1987)

The strategies of improving both planning and public choice can appear contradictory. Tensions exist within the new system between, on the one hand, the assumptions of prescribed universal entitlement (through the National Curriculum and Assessment) and, on the other hand, the variety of experience that may follow choice and competition in an educational market place (for example, open enrolment, and 'opting out' into a new grant maintained sector). This encouragement of competition through the creation of an internal market in the public sector of education complements and reinforces the policy of privatisation through competitive tendering (for example, school cleaning and grounds maintenance). Furthermore, this strategy of simultaneously centralising and decentralising government would be likely to introduce tensions into the management of the service especially for the Local Education Authority in its efforts to understand new roles and relations.

The changing role of the LEA

The LEA has, traditionally, been known as the 'maintaining authority': providing schools and colleges in order to meet the educational needs of the local population. This task of developing the institutional arrangements for local education gave LEAs, in the past, a role which increasingly placed them at the centre of the post-war government and planning of education. In responding to the post-war birth bulge with an extensive school building programme and in the years of comprehensive reorganisation LEAs preoccupied themselves with the infrastructure that would provide more opportunities for all young people to develop their potential through education. By improving the institutional context within which learning took place the LEA was providing the conditions for teachers to carry out their professional skills. Even though the LEA had responsibility for the curriculum (under section 27 of the 1944 Education Act) and for the education of the community (section 7) issues of learning process, however, were regarded typically as professional matters for heads and their staffs in schools and colleges. LEAs developed and administered the framework of education while delegating the content and quality of learning to others (Ranson and Thomas 1989). The functional responsibilities and tasks of LEA management of education are redefined by the Reforms.

- *Policy* To prepare a curriculum policy for 5–16 year old pupils and students aged 16–19 and to contribute to the implementation of the National Curriculum.
- *Planning provision* remains the responsibility of the LEA to provide schools and colleges sufficient to the local needs of the area. Thus it is the duty of the LEA ' . . . to secure that there shall be available for their area sufficient schools for providing primary education.. and for providing secondary education..offering such variety of instruction and training as may be desirable . . . ' and '..to secure the provision for their area of adequate facilities for further education'.
- *Finance and resources* It is the task of the LEA to determine overall levels of resources and the formula by which they are to be shared between institutions. The LEA retains the responsibility to manage schools with no delegated budgets.
- *Monitoring and evaluation* To inspect LEA-maintained institutions and monitor their performance in implementing the National Curriculum and to evaluate the success of LMS schemes in improving the quality of teaching and learning.

- *Sanctions* The LEA will have the power to withdraw delegated budgets from governors and institutions based upon clear educational and other grounds; encourage corrective action to prevent the need for sanctions.
- *Services to institutions* It will be the responsibility of the LEA to provide a range of support and advice to insitutions on development planning, budgeting, curricular and assessment matters, staff appointments and development, as well as information technology and building related matters. Thompson and Parison (1989) offer a helpful classification of the different relationships implied in servicing institutions:

  (i)   provision of services controlled by the LEA: for example, capital expenditure, specific grants, school inspection and home to school transport;

  (ii) provision of services where the control lies with the institution: for example, non-structural repairs and maintenance, peripatetic and advisory services, premises and equipment insurance, recruitment, advertising and selection;

  (iii) the statutory right of an LEA to offer advice and support, for example, of the chief education officer on selection and appointment matters;

  (iv) provision of advice and support where the LEA has no statutory right, for example, where the institution has the responsibility to establish and operate its own disciplinary and grievance procedures, but can ask the LEA for advice and support.

- *Services to individual pupils, students and parents* It is the duty of the LEA to continue to provide services to their clients including: admissions, secondary transfer, awards, the assessment and placement of children with special needs, and home to school transport. Services also include child guidance, careers guidance, education welfare, financial assistance.
- *Public accountability* Services to parents and the public, publishing information on admission arrangements, financial information, institutional budgets and outturns and providing information on the performance of individual schools and colleges, setting up complaints machinery and appeals procedures; advise on governors reports

Thus the tasks and responsibilities of the LEA are altered by the 1988 Education Reform Act. Yet although powers are reduced the significance of the LEA role in local education is possibly even enhanced. The Audit Commission (1989) argued as much in an occasional paper, *Losing an Empire, Finding a Role: The LEA of the Future*. The LEA would have to learn to share power and responsibilities in a more pluralist environment: upwards with the Secretary of State advised by the National Curriculum Council, the Schools Examinations and Assessment Council and other bodies; downwards with individual schools and colleges and their governors; and outwards with parents and other interested groups from the community. LEAs could discover 'rewarding' roles in the new responsibilities:

The LEA will be:

(i) a **leader**, articulating a vision of what the education service is trying to achieve;

(ii) a **partner**, supporting schools and colleges and helping them to fulfil this vision;

(iii) a **planner**, of facilities for the future;

(iv) a **provider of information**, to the education market, helping people to make informed choices;

(v) a **regulator**, of quality in schools and colleges;

(vi) a **banker**, channelling the funds which enable local institutions to deliver.

None of these roles could be neglected although different LEAs might emphasise some rather than others depending on local needs and policies. The Audit Commission paper indicated that one LEA was giving prominence to the provider of services role, while another was developing a more directive and prescriptive role, and a third LEA perceived itself as the manager of a club.

But in the view of the Commission there are some features which should be common to all strategies. In particular:

– they should all include clear statements of educational objectives;

– they should provide support for schools and colleges which allows them to progress towards an agreed level of autonomy;

– their approaches to budget setting and resource allocation should be founded on an assessment of the needs of the ultimate client relationship;

– they should incorporate monitoring information systems which are robust, useful and user-friendly.

(Audit Commission, 1989)

Thus the roles and purposes of the LEA as well as of governors and their schools or colleges in the new management of education are transformed by the reforms. Old assumptions about power and authority have to be set aside as new relationships form in a redesigned network. The prescriptions for the new ERA appear the same throughout the system: *learning quality, public accountability*, and *better management*. Indeed, better management, arguably bears the burden of the reform's effectiveness as a whole. Only improved management at the level of schools, colleges and their LEAs can create a service which ensures more effective teaching and learning as well as institutions that respond more efficiently to what their communities believe about them.

Nationalising local education

Whatever progress was made by local education authorities in adapting their role in a new system of local education a number of developments led to them being the focus of renewed critical attack and a growing clamour from the Right to nationalise education. The politics of poll tax and the pressure to reduce local bills led to speculation, from the autumn of 1990, that parts of local education would be taken over by the central Exchequer; this financial expediency together with the need to develop a coherent strategy for post sixteen education and training led to the launch of a White Paper in May, 1991 and the Schools Bill in November; and, most significantly, the slow response to opting out together with growing Government belief that of all the LEA reforms this policy held the key, has caused the Government to sanction a number of incentives to persuade more schools to seek grant maintained status. Now it seemed opting out was not just an escape valve for a few schools, but the expected course for all schools, while the LEA would be eliminated or diminished from the strategic leader of a local system to a mere service agency in the market place. Together these recent initiatives indicate the demise of the local government of education. The key components of new attack on local government will be discussed in turn.

Reducing the LEA to reduce the poll tax[1]

Local government finance has been the nightmare of governments since the early 1970s and a recurring option for reducing the burden upon the ratepayer or poll taxpayer has been to consider transferring parts or the whole of local authority educational expenditure to central government. The alternatives put forward during the winter of 1990 were for the central Exchequer to take over: teachers salaries, school expenditure, further education and post 16 colleges, and the whole education service.

(i) Transferring teachers' salaries to central government
One option for reducing local expenditure on education was to transfer the primary cost of teachers – their salaries – to central government. This option has not been chosen probably because

of the problems associated with the transfer. The most obvious dilemma for the Government would be the increased burden on central spending equivalent to 4.4 pence on the basic rate of income tax. This would be at the expense of £2.50 reduction in the average (equivalent of) poll or council tax (on the assumption that business rates were reduced proportionately as well as poll taxes.

In the short term at least, the LEAs would still have to administer the payroll and the associated functions of personnel management.

> cash would be paid by central government to LEAs for onward transmission to schools via their formulae. Schools' funding would then be subdivided between the national teaching element and LEA money for other expenditure; although schools would be able, as now, to spend their total funds as they thought fit. The alternative would be a complete lack of flexibility and a negation of the principle of delegated power to schools.
> However, the existence of central funding would establish an effective quota on teachers as each school would be allocated only sufficient funding per pupil to buy teachers at an average cost to meet a national average pupil:teacher ratio (PTR). This national benchmark would thus undermine local management, one of the central features of the Government's 1988 Education Reform Act, designed to give more power to governors. There would be a further problem of 'topping up' by LEAs. If LEAs are allowed to provide additional funds for schools to employ more teachers this would vitiate the policy and call into question the legitimacy of using poll tax revenues for this purpose. However, if schools are to retain their power of virement between individual budgets – a main plank of the local management policy – de facto topping up could not be prevented.
> (Association of Metropolitan Authorities 1991, p. 2)

The differences, moreover, between LEAs both in their levels of expenditure and in their historic PTRs, chosen to reflect local needs and priorities, would make the choice of any national average a difficult process with painful consequences for those LEAs/schools which had to 'level down'. This strategy was not taken forward.

(ii) Transferring all school expenditure to central government
This option has not yet been chosen but might be considered to follow logically from any strategy to encourage all schools to opt out. Many practical problems would follow. Many schools, while fulfilling their principal function of providing primary or secondary education, also offer a whole range of other complementary services – including nursery and adult classes – associated with a broader conception of providing education in and for the community as a whole. Special education also illustrates the complexity of institutional relationships which any simple removal of 'schools'

belies. The task of integrating children with special needs in mainstream education, promoted by the 1981 Education Act, requires careful planning between schools as well as additional support from the LEA.

Nationalising schools would make it particularly difficult for central government to maintain their present policy that formulae funding for schools should vary according to the choices of local areas. Making adjustments to 116 funding formulae would produce pressures upon the centre that would lead inexorably to the creation of one national formula for funding schools:

> Although it would be possible to roll forward existing formulae in the short term, it could not be continued indefinitely. Devising and maintaining formulae is a complex business which has not yet achieved a stable steady state. It would be difficult, or impossible, for DES civil servants, without knowledge or experience, to grapple with the problem of 116 separate formulae and the many sub-formulae that most authorities have introduced; but LEAs would have neither the funding nor the involvement to continue to do it. On the other hand, rationalisation towards a single formula covering all schools would be an administrative nightmare – apart from the politically and fiscally difficult questions of levelling up or down in the short term – and finding a workable formula that could provide adequately for all 24,000 schools without waste or under provision.
>
> (Association of Metropolitan Authorities 1991, p. 4)

The administration of specific grants would also become impossibly complicated. Since their inception in 1984, specific grants have been one of the strategies of Whitehall to influence the development of local education, LEAs having to bid for grants (for professional and curriculum development) that are determined according to criteria chosen by the Government. Without LEAs to apply for and administer these grants the DES would have to review thousands of bids from individual schools for twenty or more categories of expenditure.

Thus the administrative consequences of transferring the cost of schools to the centre would be considerable: either the LEA would be retained as a mere agency to administer the implementation of central government decision making dividing authority and accountability. Or, the LEA would have no locus in school management thus producing remote management of schools: Whitehall responsible for local planning of school places (including school reorganisations and public consultations), the review of local appeals and complaints, and many management decisions: including teacher shortages and building repairs. Responsibility for providing advice and inspecting schools would also presumably pass to the DES implying a considerable expansion of HM Inspectorate or using the existing local advisory services on an agency basis.

(iii) The transfer of expenditure on further education colleges

Of the several options available this has seemed the most attractive to central government even before the publication of the White Paper on Education and Training. Further education in England costs £1.67 billion and its transfer to central government would, it has been calculated, allow a reduction of £90 in poll tax, although adding 1.5 pence in income tax. The attractiveness of this option may derive from a superficial similarity with the transfer of the polytechnics from local control authorised by the 1988 Education Reform Act:

> It is certainly true that many FE colleges are large institutions with powerful and effective governing bodies, and the largest of them are of an equivalent size to the smaller Polytechnics and Colleges Funding Council institutions. However, their circumstances are in many ways very different. Higher education had been subject to national planning via the local authority supported National Advisory Body and had been nationally funded through a pooling system; further education colleges are still planned and funded locally.
>
> (Association of Metropolitan Authorities 1991, p. 5)

The LEA was given, under the 1988 Education Reform Act, a strategic role not only in planning and coordinating further education but in post-compulsory vocational education and training taking into account existing provision and the needs of local people as well as employers and the general requirements of local economic development. Moreover, because further education colleges have been formulae funded by LEAs the arguments against national funding formulae developed above in relation to the local management of schools would equally apply to colleges.

(iv) The complete nationalisation of education

The complete transfer of education from local to central government, proposed by at least 80 Conservative MPs who signed an Early Day Motion in 1991, would raise many issues. Levels of expenditure on education would very likely be severely reduced in many local areas. This would happen because a nationally controlled and delivered service would need a national formula to replace the 116 local formulae of LEAs. It is likely that any such formula would ensure that spending on education conforms much more closely in future to an equivalent of the present 'standard spending assessments' (SSAs) which state what central government believes local authorities should spend on particular services. There would be no local authorities to supplement the meagre expenditure allocations from Whitehall:

> If this year the government had used SSAs to determine spending on education, AMA analysis of budgets as compared with SSAs for 1990–91 shows that the Government would have needed to make cuts of over £1 billion; in other words, an average of 7% per LEA. This is the difference between the level of the Government's estimate of the needs of LEAs and the decisions made by LEAs on actual spending in their local areas. This would have meant thousands of teachers being made redundant despite teacher shortages in some areas, and funds for new books and equipment being drastically reduced.
>
> Since the average cost of a teacher (including 18 per cent on costs) is nearly £19,000 and the cost of 100 primary school text books is £300 and of 100 secondary textbooks is £500, a cut of £1 million in spending on education would mean over 500 teachers being made redundant; or textbook orders for primary schools and secondary schools being cut by 125,000 each.
>
> AMA's analysis shows that cuts of this size would have meant slashing budgets by over 5% in 73 LEAs. The highest cut would have been in Westminster where the budget would have been reduced by over 43%.
>
> (Association of Metropolitan Authorities 1991, paper 2, p. 1)

Any national formula however would undermine the Government's commitment to the *local* management of schools with governors controlling the routine management of their schools supported by the strategic role of the LEA including the formula itself designed to reflect the local character and needs of schools and the communities they serve. Brought into question would be the newly created authority and responsibility of school governors to determine how they should spend their budget, 'viring' money if necessary between budget heads.

In summarising these options for transferring all or part of educational expenditure to central government, it is clear that educational expenditure has not yet been nationalised although the proposals contained in the White Paper together with the incipient trend to opting out may in time have the same effect. The discussion here has suggested a number of consequences of nationalising educational expenditure:

- increase the burden on the tax payer at least to the same extent as any reduction in poll tax;
- control of educational expenditure (more) directly from Whitehall would lead to large scale cuts in parts of the country;
- any new administrative arrangements (perhaps regional) would be likely to be more remote and unresponsive to local

needs than at present. Would any such a national system have the capacity to respond quickly and flexibly to local changes in need, for example the migration of families and the consequent changes in community pattern?

– the transitional arangements would be disruptive and cause inefficiencies.

It is unlikely that any such nationalised system would do away with all local adminstration but local democracy would be the casualty of any system to replace the present local government of education. The creation of education or school boards for areas or regions would reproduce the LEA, but bereft of its present democratic responsibilities and revenue raising powers. And in local government (assuming it survived) there would be the strange arrangement whereby local councillors were elected to represent their constituents needs but were unable to contribute to or influence directly in any way the local schools and colleges.

The White Paper on education and training for the 21st century

On 21 March 1991, the Government announced its intention that the FE colleges would be given independent corporate status and be funded direct by an FE funding council from April 1993. Within a couple of months this idea provided the platform for a much more far reaching and extensive initiative. On 20 May, 1991 the Prime Minister launched a major programme of reform of post compulsory education and training for the 21st century. Its primary objectives are: to ensure that virtually the whole of the 16–19 age group are drawn into education and training; to reform post-16 qualifications; to raise the status of vocational studies; and to provide employers with a dominating voice in the new system.

The White Papers in effect create a new 16–18 college sector of education. From 1 April 1993, colleges of further education together with tertiary and sixth form colleges will be given independent corporate status and form a new directly funded sector focusing upon the needs of over two million full and part-time students. (Colleges with less than 15 per cent of students on roll who are full-time, day release and block release students, will remain with the local authorities. Any sixth form college which opts for grant maintained status before 1993 will also become part of the new sector.) It is believed that in time most of the current distinctions between different types of colleges will disappear as, for example, sixth form colleges take on vocational courses and part-time students.

The colleges will become a legally independent corporate body with powers: to provide education for those over 16; to employ their own staff; to enter into contracts on their own behalf; to manage assets and resources, and to act otherwise as a legal body undertaking activities in furtherance of their purposes as providers of education . . .

With charitable status funded through two councils, one each for England and Wales and advised, in England, by (7 to 10) regional advisory committees with offices and staff, these new councils, with strong industrial, commercial and professional representation, will be appointed by the Education Secretary in consultation with the Employment Secretary. They will have wide ranging powers and responsibilities for the new sector, including the planning of provision, incorporating the power to determine what kind of courses colleges should offer, controlling the allocation of annual funding as well as capital resources, and monitoring the quality of college performance.

The LEAs will have only a tenuous link with the new college sector, being asked merely to *liaise* with the colleges while local councillors will only be able to serve on the governing bodies of the colleges if invited to do so. The Government, some have interpreted, 'is determined to ensure a complete rupture between the colleges and their present masters (*Times Educational Supplement* 24 May, 1991, p. 4). The TECS, however, are to be accorded the right to become governors.

> After the reforms instruments of government will no longer provide for formal LEA representation. The legislation will, however, remove the provision in the 1988 Education Reform Act which prevents people who are local authority members or employees from being co-opted on to governing bodies. Governing bodies will be able to co-opt two additional members. This means that some governors may well combine their public service on the governing body with membership of a local authority. They will be co-opted for their individual qualities, and not as delegates or representatives of the local authority . . .
>
> Existing employment interest governors should be supplemented by a representative of a local TEC. This will reflect the TECs' important contribution to training locally and their increasing involvement in vocational education.

The colleges will be funded in part from an education and training council grant. This will comprise two components: a cash limited block grant together with a further amount based upon student admissions. Colleges will continue to derive funds from: TEC grants under the work-related further education programme, grants from polytechnics if they undertake some higher education work; fee income from employers and students; and from consultancy and other services. The colleges will be able to offer training credits, which are vouchers for 16 or 17 year olds to pay for part-time vocational education and training. The scheme will be managed by the TECs. Now being piloted in eleven areas of the country, the White Paper proposes that by 1996 all 16 or 17 year olds will be offered training credits to pay for vocational education and training.

The careers service, the White Paper recommends, should improve the quality of its work and become more responsive to the needs of employers so that young people can take advantage of the opportunities currently being developed. But, 'These new goals require a new way of organising the careers service, particularly if closer cooperation with employers is to be secured'. LEAs, at present, manage the careers service locally, but this responsibility seems likely to disappear in any ensuing legislation, with the Government proposing to take the service wholly or partly out of the hands of local authorities. In the mean time they are to be encouraged voluntarily to set up partnerships with the TECs to manage the service jointly. The options for future management include: the transfer of some responsibilities to the TECs; handing the careers service over wholly to the TECs; requiring LEAs to contract out their careers work to the private sector.

This wide ranging reconstituting of the governance of post-16 education and training is designed to support reforms which will ostensibly break down the divide between academic and vocational system of learning and qualification. A vocationally oriented competence based curriculum and assessment is to be given parity of esteem with the academic:

> Young people and adults need a clear framework of qualifications to measure their success in education and training. We need to build up a modern system of academic and vocational qualifications which are equally valued. They must both set a high standard and offer ladders of opportunity after sixteen and throughout working life . . .
>
> Vocational qualifications in this country have been undervalued and underused. A major reform is underway to produce clear, nationally recognised qualifications. The reform is led by the National Council for Vocational Qualifications . . . the NCVQ should work with others to develop criteria for accrediting more vocational qualifications.

At the same time, a framework of principles will be designed to ensure the quality off all A-level and AS syllabuses. New diplomas will encompass these academic (eg A-levels) and vocational (NVQ) qualifications. The Government intends that these principles should control the development of syllabuses, limiting assessment by coursework and establishing examinations at the end of courses as the norm. Other changes include:

- School sixth forms to be allowed to admit part-time and adult students, and to accept training credits or to charge fees for them.
- Education compacts to be extended nation wide; these are bargains between young people, employers and colleges. Young people work towards personal goals and in return employers provide a job with training for those who achieve their goals.
- Vocational adult education to be funded through colleges; leisure/social adult education expected to be funded by fees.

Local authorities and the teacher associations have been critical about the implications of the White Paper for: firstly, the development of coherent strategies and plans for the post compulsory education and training which had been at the centre of the 1988 Education Reform Act; secondly, the narrow, utilitarian conception of the purposes of education and training; and thirdly, special educational needs post-16. The influence of the TECs and a tendency to output measurement of performance were already leaving students and trainees with SEN at the margin. *The Times Educational Supplement* concluded that 'even if reducing local taxation is no longer an electoral imperative, the Government is going out of its way to strip the local authorities of responsibility or influence in further education and its support services' (24 May 1991, p. 4).

Marginalising the LEA through opting out

Grant maintained schools (GMS) lie at the centre of the new right ideological thrust of the Government's education policy, embodying a belief that institutions can stand alone and especially free from the influence of the local education authority which is typically cast as a malign influence upon schools and colleges. Stuart Maclure (1988), the former editor of the *Times Educational Supplement* was clear about the intention of the opting out provisions of the Education Reform Act: 'No provision in the Act aroused stronger feelings than those on grant maintained schools. The aim was to break the local authorioties monopoly of maintained schooling – the provision of free schools, paid for out of public funds' (p. 56). The Government's consultation paper July 1987:

> The Government is taking action to increase the autonomy of schools and their responsiveness to parental wishes . . .
> The Government considers that it should also respond to the numerous indications it has received that groups of parents want the responsibility of running their schools as individual institutions. It proposes to provide

an additional route to autonomy by introducing legislation later this year to enable the governors of county and voluntary maintained schools, with the support of the parents, to apply to the Secretary of State for maintenance by grant from Central Government instead of maintenance by LEAs. The Government believes that this proposal . . . will add a new and powerful dimension to the ability of parents to exercise choice within the publicly provided sector of education. The greater diversity of provision which will result should enhance the prospect of improving education standards in all schools. Parents and local communities would have new opportunities to secure the development of their schools in ways appropriate to the needs of their children and in accordance with their wishes, within the legal framework of a national curriculum.

(DES, July 1987)

The schools eligible to apply for grant maintained status include all secondary schools and primary schools with over 300 pupils, but not nursery or small primary schools. GM schools would thus form a new type of maintained school, providing free education although like LEA schools they would be able to accept voluntary donation from parents and others in the community. GM schools would not be able to undergo a change of character or any significant change in their size or age range at the same time as the change to grant maintained status:

It is the Secretary of State's intention that schools should retain their previous character as LEA schools so that, for example, a comprehensive school would remain comprehensive . . . that the character of the school would be maintained as reflected in the school's admissions policy.

(DES, July 1987)

It was expected that most GM schools would require a period to establish themselves in their new role before contemplating any major changes. When such a change was contemplated the GM school would, like LEA schools, need to publish statutory proposals to allow public consultation.

A distinctive and elaborate statutory procedure was proposed to enable the constituting of GM schools. An application for GM status should have the consent of a parental ballot. Any decision of the governors to hold such a ballot has to be confirmed at two meetings of the governing body. The process was set out in the 1988 Education Reform Act:

S60 (1) In the case of any school which is eligible for grant maintained status, a ballot of parents on the question of whether grant-maintained status should be sought for the school shall be held in accordance with section 61 of this Act if either-

(a) the governing body decide by a resolution passed at a meeting of that body ('the first resolution') to hold such a ballot and confirm

that decision . . . by a resolution ('the second resolution') passed
at a subsequent meeting of the governing body held not less than
twenty eight days, nor more than forty-two days, after that at which
the first resolution was passed; or
(b) they receive a written request to hold such a ballot which meets
the requirements of subsection (2) below.

(2) Those requirements are that the request must be signed (or
otherwise endorsed in such a manner as the governing body may
require) by a number of parents of registered pupils at the school
equal to at least twenty per cent of the number of registered pupils
at the school on the date which the request is received . . .

S.61   (8) Where in the case of any ballot held in respect of a school
in accordance with this section other than the one held by virtue of
this subsection ('the first ballot') the total number of votes cast in the
ballot by persons elligible to vote in the ballot is less than fifty per
cent of the number of persons so elligible, it shall be the duty of the
governing body to secure that another ballot ('the second ballot') is
held before the end of the period of fourteen days beginning with
the date immediately following that on which the result of the first
ballot is determined.

The second vote is decided by a simple majority. If the vote is in
favour of opting out then the governors have six months in which
to publish their proposals for the acquisition of grant maintained
status, submitting a copy to the Secretary of State.

Legislation determined that if the application was approved by
the Secretary of State the budget of the new GM school would
be provided by the Department of Education and Science (DES)
but would be determined according to the same formulae as if it
had remained as an LEA school together with an allocation which
represented the DES' view of what the school should receive to
cover its due proportion of the LEA's costs of central services (which
'fairly represents what the LEA would have spent on provision at
the school and on the provision of central services and benefits').
Further grants would be paid to GM schools: 'Special purpose'
grants to meet any special needs of the population of the area
served by the school (including money for urban aid or Section
11 tasks), together with expenditure on staffing and INSET; and
grants to cover capital expenditure.

On 30 June 1988 Mr Baker, the Secretary of State, when issuing
a draft of guidance on GM schools commented that 'the advent of
GM schools will provide the opportunity for parents and the local
community to run their own schools. Increased scope for choice
between schools is not only desirable in itself but will in turn help
to improve standards in all our schools' (DES 192/88).

Much interest was expressed in the criteria that would be used
to approve grant maintained schools. Publicly, the Government

indicated that such schools would have to be well established and successul schools, in terms of numbers (especially in the sixth form), with educationally successful performance indicators; experience of managing school budgets; and widespread support for opting out from parents as well as the governors and the staff.

Yet there appeared to be differences of view even within Government about whether grant maintained schools would be a limited sector of schools (gaining in time the prestige of the old direct grant grammar schools) or whether preferred policy indicated that in time GM schools would be the norm with most or all schools opted out, with the Secretary of State willing to accept schools with marginal poll victories in order to accelerate the trend to opting out.

Implementing the policy
A summary analysis of the evidence of the schools which have (at November 1991) been involved in the public stages of the opting out procedures indicates that:

- 135 schools have been approved for GM status (102 are operating as such);
- 236 schools out of 26,000 schools in England and Wales (until 1990, only 6,700 schools were eligible to opt out) formally voted in favour, have published proposals; had proposals approved; or are now operating as GM schools;
- 46 of the 236 are primary schools;
- 45 of the 236 are subject to reorganisation proposals;
- 167 of the 236 are county council schools;
- 47 of the 236 are London schools;
- 155 of the 236 are in Conservative councils (65.7%);
- 49 of the 236 are in Labour councils (20.8%);
- 32 of the 236 are in hung councils (13.6%).

Any adequate interpretive analysis of opting out will need to await the evidence of those research programmes which are specialising on opting out – in particular further data on voting in governor and parental ballots as well as decision making by different Secretaries of State, together with an understanding of the motives of the different parties to the politics of opting out. Nevertheless, the evidence available at this stage suggests that:

- many of the schools seeking and achieving opt out status have been the subject of reorganisation proposals to rationalise surplus places (in accord with government policy) and have thus been threatened with closure or amalgamation;
- a significant proportion of the early proposals for GM status have been from grammar schools. In October 1990 of the

48 schools which had won approval for GM status, 21 were grammar schools;
- a major proportion of the support for opting out (167/236) has come from schools in county councils. More research is needed to discover what this indicates: perhaps a greater tradition of autonomy from the LEA; perhaps counties have been slower than metropolitan authorities in rationalising surplus places – 26/45 of the schools facing reorganisation proposals and receiving positive support for or accomplishing opting out are in county councils;
- the proportion of schools opting out of Conservative LEAs is much greater than Labour LEAs: once more further research is needed to identify why this is: part of this reason will overlap with the county issues; part may have to do with budgets that are more constrained than in metropolitan areas;
- there is a relationship between opting out and low spending by LEAs (spending close to standard spending assessment government guidelines (SSAs) (Ranson 1991, Rogers 1991);
- nearly half the schools opting out have failed to secure an absolute majority of parents.

It has been difficult to interpret, in the Secretary of State's decisions, any application of consistent criteria about whether schools should be allowed to opt out. The Department of Education and Science has been criticised for being unwilling to publish its criteria. Mr Clarke, the Secretary of State, turned down the opt out proposal of Walsingham School in Wandsworth even though 96 per cent of parents had voted in favour, while the Minister was willing to accept only 51.3 per cent of parents in support of the proposal for Newham's Stratford School to opt out. Grant maintained status was similarly accorded to schools in Avon and Warwickshire which were subject to reorganisation proposals. Furthermore, whereas Walsingham was refused permission, with a role of 750 pupils, the Warwickshire school, Newbold Grange was accepted with a roll of 300 pupils: a school which the local authority believed failed the Government's own criteria of viability will it is believed, become the smallest GM school.

The Government's opt out policy has not, so far, been the success the Government might have wished for it. The movement towards opting out has been slow, a number of the schools have been earmarked for closure, thus creating confusion between government policies: on the one hand encouraging LEAs to plan to take out surplus places and thus close schools, while on the other hand allowing schools to survive so as to create a new sector to compete with the old.

The response of Government has been to step up their commitment to the opt out policy and to promote incentives to persuade those caught in two minds. In October 1990 Mr MacGregor, the Secretary of State, described the right to opt out as 'the jewel in the crown of parent power' and stated that he would lift the restriction preventing primary schools with fewer than 300 pupils from leaving local authority control. Schools would also have their transitional grants doubled and a broad hint was given that the balloting procedure would be streamlined.

Increasing the incentives for schools to opt out would be a significant change of policy because the Government had from the outset claimed that GM schools would be treated no more favourably over funding than schools remaining in local authority control.

It is the clear policy of the Secretary of State, that schools should be encouraged to opt out. Indeed the Prime Minister has admitted recently that it has been the tacit policy of the Government to provide incentives to persuade schools to opt out. There have arguably been incentives, despite protestations to the contrary, since the legislation was first enacted: schools benefitted from:

- a small start up grant;
- a staff restructuring grant: an unspecified amount to be bid for;
- a specific grant for development: for the costs of management and teacher training and implementation of the national curriculum, of £41 per pupil;
- a capital grant by bidding to the DES; an increased chance of finance for building improvements; and
- a share of discretionary exceptions; that is receiving directly the cash equivalent of that proportion of the cost of running the school which the LEA had previously incurred (for example, for the provision of advisory services, school meals, administration of payroll, personnel, finance, curriculum support as well as other support services). In Kent, for example, this was 13 per cent of the schools' general budget.

Now, these incentives have been dramatically increased since the autumn of 1990 to step up the pressures on schools to join the GM sector: these have been:

1. In October 1990, the Secretary of State announced that all primary schools could apply for grant maintained status.
2. At the same time he announced increases in the start up grant, so that primary schools could receive £15,000–£30,000 extra according to size (together with the transitional grant of £30 per

pupil), while secondary schools could receive £40,000 according to size (plus £30 per pupil). This is of course particularly attractive to small secondary schools which are often persuaded to consider opting out in order to survive.

While Ministers have conceded that schools opting out would receive at least three times as big a maintenance grant as council controlled schools, some critics have proposed that the differential could be five times as big.

3. High probability of capital grant. Indeed it has been argued that the DES favours grant maintained schools in the capital programme, such that the chances of obtaining building grants are considerably greater for GM schools and this includes grants for building improvement, a category not available to LEA schools. In 1989/90 £6.6m was allocated to the first 29 opt out schools, and in 1990/91 £10.5m has been allocated to the first 56 GM schools (while £472m has been allocated to more than 5,000 LEA secondary schools):

- the largest allocation is £1.5m to a grammar school in Cheltenham, while a Tameside school which received half a million pounds last year is to receive a further £0.25m this year;
- in one London Borough, £1.5m will be spent in support of a struggling school.

Although the Department of Education and Science has disputed the figures presented by the Labour Party that opt-out schools receive nearly four times as much funding for building work as schools remaining with LEAs (that is £326 per pupil for GM schools compared with £83 per pupil in neighbouring schools) nevertheless the DES has conceded that expenditure levels for opt out schools engaged in building projects are running at two and a half times the allocation in the maintained sector (£240 a pupil compared with £100).

4. For all LEAs a flat rate addition of 16 per cent of the central administration costs of the AMG is to be allocated to opted out schools; following LEA pressure the Government reduced this figure to 15 per cent in October 1991 and proposed that LEAs could apply for further reductions in the grant they lose where more than one in seven of their primary or secondary schools has opted out.

5. In April, 1991 the Government abandoned the 5 year restriction on schools which opt out from being able to change their character (say to grammar school).

6. Privacy about performance of public GM schools; opted out schools are not subject to public inspections.

7. The debt burden is left behind with the LEA which has to continue to pay off previous investment in opted out schools even though they no longer receive a central government grant for them. Thus local people are continuing to pay off investment in schools they no longer control.

Points not included in essay - are v. imp.

The Education (Schools) Bill[2]

The presentation of the Schools Bill (6 November 1991) increased fears that the role of the LEA established by the 1988 Education Reform Act was gradually being diminished. The responsibility of assuring the quality of school performance was being eroded. The Bill, gave effect to proposals outlined in *The Citizen's Charter* White Paper (July, 1991) to improve the provision of information about the performance of schools and to introduce regular and independent inspection of schools. The shock contained in the Bill was that LEAs would lose the statutory power of inspecting their own schools. A new role was proposed for HMI, largely to preside over a system of registered inspectors, who could tender for school inspections to be commissioned by governing bodies. The focus of LEA concern was the proposed repeal of s. 77(3) of the Education Act 1944 (the LEA's powers to inspect), together with the requirement that, if LEA inspectors were to inspect schools, that would have to be by successfully tendering for the job.

Consultations on these proposals ended ten days *after* the Bill had been given First Reading. The Second Reading debate, on 19 November, produced no soothing words for LEAs, whose inspectors were condemned in, amongst other passages, the Secretary of State's quotation of a critique by the Secondary Heads Association. Mr. Clarke also made some more generalised attacks on authorities stewardship of educational standards. Again doubt fell on the 1988 dispensations.

Removal of the power to inspect, underlined by transfer of resources for inspection to schools to fund the new contractors, appeared to cut the evaluatory function of the LEA. If s. 77 (3) were to go, then most of the legal justifications for the LEAs continuation as schools authority depended on the enabling powers of s.111 of the Local Government Act 1972, and what might be inferred from such duties as those of the employer, maintainer of the structures of buildings, overseer of teachers appraisal, and budget spender of last resort. How to discharge the 1944 Act's duty to secure efficient education (s.7) in sufficient and adequately equipped schools (s. 8) suddenly looked problematic.

Conclusion

Although the 1988 Education Reform Act withdrew powers from the local education authority it nevertheless accorded it, potentially a leading role in the implementation of the reforms with major reponsibilities for strategy and quality assurance. There is evidence that many LEAs have been responding with skill and enthusiasm to the new role. Yet before enough time has elapsed to implement adequately the reforms, the LEA has once more become the focus of critical attack and the Government has embarked on policies which can only lead to the local government of education 'withering on the vine'.

The decisions presage the nationalising of education. The preoccupation with reducing the levels of local expenditure on education, the White Paper's centralising of control of post-16 education and training, and the regeneration of the flagging policy on opting out, will together have the effect of marginalising and eroding local government in education. The decisions imply a reversal of policies legislated for in 1988 – withdrawing the strategic role of the LEA in further education – and a denial of ministerial commitment that, for example, opted out schools would be treated no more favourably than LEA schools.

The decisions reflect a preoccupation with reducing local public expenditure on education, a search to strengthen the power of Whitehall over education and the final domination of a distinctive set of values about the governance of education – that education should be provided in autonomous and competing institutions, supported if necessary only by a limited service agency, and governed from Whitehall. The uneasy balance of traditions in the 1988 Education Reform Act between the tradition of partnership and the new era of public choice and competition is now being resolved with the evident demise of the role of local government in education.

How have local authorities responded first to the challenge set them by the 1988 Education Reform Act and the recent turning of the screw against them? The discussion now turns to the initiatives in four local education authorities.

Notes

[1] This section draws heavily upon public papers prepared by the Association of Metropolitan Authorities in their defence of local government in 1991. I am grateful to their education officer for sending me the papers and giving me permission to use them in this book.

[2] This section is informed by a note to the author from the education officer of the AMA).

Part 2   Local authority perspectives on the reform of education

3
London Borough of Enfield For partnership in the learning LEA

PART 1 1988–90

Anticipating the reforms

Enfield anticipated the movement of Government policy long before the 1988 legislative reforms and began their planning accordingly. 'We anticipated the changes in the Education Reform Act and the trend towards the weakening of LEA powers and the creation of more independent schools. It gave us thinking time, to review what would be the basic role of the LEA and to develop a number of systems to prepare for the changes. I thought that schools would be vulnerable with these changes and that we would need to develop support for schools and to encourage schools to learn to support each other. It also presupposed that there was ability in the institutions as well as a changed role for the LEA – not a centre dominating and controlling, but rather trying to develop collaborative practice. Schools, colleges and the LEA should work together in partnership' (CEO).

This strategy, however, formed a natural extension of ideas and policies which had been unfolding in Enfield since the late 1970s. The Director believed that it would be a twenty year task to develop the Borough's education service. There has been a clear conception of its architecture and the foundations upon which it would need to be constructed. The first priority was to build up the resource base and this took nearly three years to develop the staffing and finances for the service. Then there were two overlapping and interdependent phases of further infrastructural development. One was to plan the reorganisation and rationalisation of the Borough's schools. This was accomplished by 1983 and led to a collegiate system for sixteen to nineteen year olds. 'It meant that we got the reorganisation out of the way while other LEAs were still half paralysed. The effect was that secondary teachers were freed from the worry of schools having to compete with each other to survive, that it would not be in their interests to cooperate because they might fear they would lose out.' Released from this anxiety the basis for cooperative working between schools and teachers was established.

The second and overlapping development during the early 1980s was the formation of a Curriculum Initiatives Group. The Director had been pressing for a curriculum statement, to clarify the purposes and stages of learning. Circular 6/81 provided the impetus for this although it was argued that any such statement should embrace the service as a whole as well as schools. The Department won a small amount of money, about £16,000 which paid for the release of teachers and others to form a curriculum 'think tank'. The members of this group were 'hand picked' by the LEA rather than being given to them as representatives of this or that group within the service. This forum, in time, introduced CPVE and prepared the development plan for TVEI.

A distinctive style of consultation and collaborative working defined each stage of development and contributed to their success. The consultation for the reorganisation exercise was undertaken by the heads: 'we informed, discussed and coached the heads. There was honesty in the consultative process and getting the heads to do it made the parents treat the exercise with utmost seriousness.' The collegiate system that resulted meant that the value of cooperative working was spelt out structurally. This emphasis upon collaboration was reinforced in the Curriculum Initiatives Group by involving a number of educational services and expecting them to work together to common solutions. A distinctive perspective on the value of partnership in shaping the purpose and organisation of the service has developed out of this experience and formed a further phase of development.

The partnership scheme

Partnership expresses both the underlying values which inform the service in Enfield as well as a specific scheme intended to encourage cooperation between schools. The overall philosophy is articulated by the CEO:

> Partnership in many forms underpins the Education Service in Enfield where there is an emphasis on inter-dependence, shared responsibility and collective action. To be successful partnership needs to be based on mutual respect, a shared responsibility, and a wish to help others to develop. This requires confidence and trust. To cooperate successfully schools need to be confident enough to have permeable boundaries. In contrast to schools which are not confident which will erect barriers to prevent the easy flow of ideas. The partnership scheme is intended to bring schools together in an organised, cooperative system which enables the schools to support each other and the LEA to support the schools.

The partnership scheme has developed in phases. The first phase was an attempt to help individual secondary schools and colleges cope with what then seemed like an unprecedented rate of change with the development of TVEI and CPVE. Each institution had a pair of 'critical friends' which meant that the management team of each school or college had access to sympathetic, external counsellors. With the introduction of institutional development plans, primary schools were grouped together to enable the Education Department to provide them with support. Reflecting upon these innovations, the CEO commented that:

> these arrangements worked very well when the headteacher and senior management team of the school were open and confident and the critical friends were also confident and energetic. Some pairs of officers and advisers were able to make good progress even when conditions inside the school were less than ideal. In some cases, inevitably, the combination of an unwillingness by the school to recognise the need to discuss its aims, objectives and programme of work and a cynical disbelief in the value of partnership on the part of some officers and advisers, proved negative and unrewarding. Some headteachers found it difficult to accept that the partnership pair should have access to heads of departments and other staff. Above all the lack of time and conflicting priorities made it difficult to ensure consistency.

In 1987/88 a second phase of partnership was inaugurated in order to develop a more effective network of cooperation and support for schools so that they could cope with the impending legislation 'even if the LEA were weakened or abolished. In this sense it was always intended as an alternative way to manage and administer the education system. The essential difference was that groups of schools would offer each other support and would work together with the help of the Education Department, although it was hoped that the tasks of organising and convening a partnership group would rest with the schools.

During this phase, the schools were clustered into 'partnership groups' although it was acknowledged that institutions would form other clusters for specific purposes. Time and resources were allocated to the groups to support their collaboration: an allocation of 0.6 teaching time as well as additional time given to each school for curriculum development and in-service training. The aims of the partnership scheme at this stage were to:

1. cope with the pressure of rapid change through mutual support and informal consultancy;
2. secure progression from one phase of education to another;
3. support curriculum development and evaluation;
4. share expertise, knowledge and skills;
5. lighten the workload by sharing common tasks;
6. share resources, such as reprographic equipment;
7. offer better support to children with special educational needs;
8. strengthen pastoral care;
9. provide a framework for INSET on a group basis;
10. support the induction of teachers new to the Borough;
11. train and develop governors;
12. provide an information network;
13. serve as an effective means of communication.

Further progress was made during this phase. 'Nevertheless . . . development has still been inconsistent. In particular, some head-teachers, officers and advisers have not seen it as a priority. Above all the lack of documentation has made it difficult for new members of staff to grasp the full potential of the scheme.'

The third phase of the partnership scheme began in September 1990, with the intention to emphasise the potential of the scheme as a framework within which schools and the LEA together can improve the quality of education following the Education Reform Act:

- for a system of evaluation and review in which schools and the LEA work together;
- assessment for key stages 1/2 and possibly 3, SEAC believes that those schools which are organised in clusters will be at an advantage;

- the appraisal of teachers
- the focus for providing professional and administrative support to schools

'Partnership must be seen as a different way of approaching schools rather than as an extra set of activities'. A distinctive structure has been developed for the Partnerships. There are five partnership support teams each serving two groups of schools. The teams comprise between six and ten officers and advisers, reflecting the different sizes of the school groups they serve, and are led jointly by a senior adviser and a schools sector education officer. There are ten partnership groups each comprising one or more secondary schools and their associated primary schools, as well as special schools and other key establishments. The groups vary in size from six to fourteen establishments. Each group will have an adviser or officer to act as its coordinator, drawn from within its partnership team. Various sub-groups may exist, the most common being the primary 'cluster'. This will have a convenor, though much of the organisational activity will be undertaken by one of the primary heads. Each establishment within a partnership group will have a single, named link person (an officer or adviser) as its primary source of contact for partnership purposes. Beyond the immediate partnership, many other sections of the education department are to reorganise to provide named links for each establishment. This means that each partnership team (and each link person) can draw on the combined resources of a wider specialist support 'team' who are in constant contact with the establishments involved.

Though the partnership scheme is central to the development of the education service it cannot carry out all the roles of the LEA and needs to be supported by a context of strategic management: through the education management team, the curriculum committee, the resources committee, and the policy units that are set up to coordinate policy across the service. It is appreciated that if the partnership scheme is to be successful it will require time and training over a three year implementation period.

Management by networks

Enfield's commitment to partnership as the necessary response to the local government of education following the Reform Act is underpinned by a philosophy of management that is particularly appropriate to a service now characterised by 'loosely-coupled' organisations. A model of management by networks expresses an approach to the way semi-autonomous organisations can relate to each other to achieve shared purposes.

Each member of the department, for example, operates in three 'domains' – a 'base' or 'home cell', a policy unit and a partnership team. The home cell provides everyone with their main (formal) designation and 'identity', but they may perform different roles in other 'domains'.

Thus within the network forums and processes are developed which allow a more differentiated service – of schools, colleges, services and the department – to come together to work out common policies and strategies for the management of the service. Network management, if it is to be successful, requires distinctive skills and understanding on the part of all who work within the network:

> Working within networks is by no means straightforward and under-standing your responsibilities within them can take time: it can be difficult to track people down, you need to trust that things are done, groups spawn other groups (and our map of groups is still incomplete).
> Networks rest on trust and if you trust you take risks. It means that guidelines are imprecise. Some do complain that they are undersupported, that the guidelines are unclear and that there are no rules. Some individuals do need rules, so there needs to be enough structure to provide this support.There is the strain of wanting to be involved, but you can't be everywhere. There is not yet sufficient reliance, trust, in individuals to get on and complete a task.
> Essentially, networks will thrive by encouraging free, bold, spirits and by continually returning to the value system – my focus is upon developing the shared value system throughout the system. The management team has to be the guardian of the value system, reaffirming and testing the values. That is the purpose of team work – to develop the values rather than specific 'decisions' alone.

The Chief Education Officer associated much of the success of the networking to the preponderance of women in key positions of the service. Their teamwork, valuing of cooperation and good inter-personal skills were an essential condition for effective networking.

Roles and responsibilities of the LEA

Within the network, each part of the service will have its own distinctive roles and responsibilities to contribute. Enfield believes that the LEA, following the Education Reform Act, has a clear role in planning, coordination and evaluation.

(i) Planning and coordination
The LEA must determine the overall pattern of provision, but it should do so through a process of assessing what pupils and

students, parents, employers and the local community expect from the service, as all are in different ways and to different degrees in the position of customers, whose needs must be identified, considered and met as far as this is practicable. This will be best achieved between the LEA and institutions working as partners, though the LEA should now view heads and governors as customers to whom the authority has to provide efficient and effective services.

Planning is essential to this process of partnership and service. Institutions will produce 'institutional development plans' (IDPs) which prioritise curriculum and staff development together with resource needs and capital programes. These plans inform and are informed by LEA plans which together allow the service to develop in a coherent way the curriculum, staffing, training and building needs. The LEA is preparing a three year plan connected to the authority's business plan.

(ii) Liaison and cooperation

The LEA will retain responsibility for overall liaison and negotiation with a wide range of bodies and groups including government departments, employers, parents, governing bodies and community groups.

(iii) Management and administration

While responsibility for many decisions is being transferred to governing bodies and to headteachers, nevertheless the overall responsibility still rests with the LEA which must find ways of ensuring that the system is managed in a coherent way through agreed plans, policies and procedures rather than through detailed controls. This will require a computerised management information system; appropriate training programmes; good procedures; and, especially, effective policies and procedures:

The LEA's influence will depend to a considerable extent on the success with which it is able to set out its policies in a clear, published form, which can be easily understood and used by staff, governors and others concerned with the service. Where policy statements reflect accurately the needs of schools and best practices to be found, they have a powerful effect. This means it is important for schools to share in their preparation and formulation wherever possible.

The LEA must further develop its role in providing well organised advice and support for institutions and their governors. Classroom teachers will need continued support, schools and colleges will need specific help on matters depending on the LEA to coordinate expertise. 'At the same time officers and advisers must act as consultants, helping institutions and their governing bodies to cope with their responsibilities in a period of rapid change'. The LEA also emphasises, as described above, that institutions should look to each other for mutual support through the partnership scheme, as well as to the LEA directly.

Enfield believes it will still be possible for the LEA, through LMS, to continue its role as a catalyst for new initiatives. 'This will be of great importance because it will allow the LEA to continue, although on a reduced scale, to pilot new developments and to test new approaches in a controlled way'.

(iv) Provider of direct services
The LEA will continue to provide a number of services directly to schools and parents. To schools, the LEA will offer administrative, financial, legal and personnel services while other services, such as cleaning and catering, will depend upon the outcome of competitive tendering. To parents, the LEA will continue to be responsible for a wide range of services affecting individual children such as child guidance, careers guidance, education welfare, meeting special educational needs, transport, and financial assistance where necessary.

(v) Monitoring and evaluation
The National Curriculum and LMS oblige the LEA to monitor and evaluate the performance of schools within a national framework. The LEA wishes to develop with schools an agreed set of performance indicators. It is hoped that groups of schools will work together with officers and advisers to develop an effective system for evaluating performance. Given such a system 'the LEA could use the process of inspection as a means of checking the effectiveness of the systems it had created rather than as the main means of evaluating the work of a school'. The LEA will be developing a process of appraisal and assessment of individual teachers as well as pupils.

The LEA believes that although the radical changes implemented by the ERA 'reduce the powers of the LEA it enhances its responsibilities because it is clear that without a vigorous and determined lead by the LEA the process of reform will founder.' The role of the LEA, therefore, is perceived as crucial to the management of change and Enfield believes, because of the changes introduced over the decade, it is well placed to respond to the demands of change – as long as resources are provided for the additional burdens upon the local education system. It is to the process of managing change that the discussion now turns.

The management of change

Enfield has responded positively to the ERA legislation perceiving opportunities to strengthen the way the service develops and is managed.

we are responding to a 'force majeur' by taking institutions into our value system which promotes cooperation, collaboration and consultation.
We take from Central Government and distil what is important for this LEA. If we are confident in what we think and believe, we can cope. We can turn the ERA into a 'house system' for us. The important thing is to know what we want to do. This enables us to select from the DES' specific grants, so that we are not at the mercy of the civil servants' bright ideas. Civil servants' like specific grants: the task for us is to use them as we want to meet our purposes. This indicates the maturity in our system and of the people who have developed over time within it.

The management of change in the LEA, therefore, is designed to clarify the values and purposes of Enfield – partnership in the development of learning quality and the creation of a strategic planning framework that will carry these values into practice.

Strategic planning

Though Enfield is committed to a new role of enabling local school partnerships it also believes that a condition for their success is the leadership the LEA must exercise through strategic planning. A three year strategic planning process has been developed, linked to the Council's financial plan, which strives to 'establish an effective and flexible planning system for the maintenance and development of the education service incorporating monitoring and evaluation procedures as an aid to the regular review of policies'. The framework for strategic planning sets out:

1. To devise and maintain a realistic and attainable three year action plan that will enable the service to realise the aims established for programme areas by undertaking systematic and critical examinations of service areas and policies to ensure their relevance to the committee's aims, to assess their long term impact and value and to consider any alternative means of service delivery; establishing systems to monitor progress and evaluate the effectiveness of action plans by defining appropriate measures of achievement within key result areas; communicating and publicising the plan to chief

officers management team; developing further a formalised communications network with staff, educational establishments, trade unions, and customers in order to facilitate consultation and gain understanding, acceptance and commitment to the action plans as well as using the process to provide intelligence to assist in evaluation; developing a coordinated approach to management information systems in order to provide improved and relevant data collection and access to information, thereby enabling better informed decisions to be made.

2. To develop the planning and review process by ensuring that accountability for the implementation of action plans and the effective use of allocated resources is made clear; and ensuring that resources are adequate to achieve planned results.

3. To forecast the need for physical resources in response to changing populations, external demands, curriculum, and advancing technology

The three year plan forms a substantial document which establishes for the period the aims of the education service; the key result areas for which are established policy priorities and performance targets, and strategy statements and action plans

Policy priorities

The strategic planning process in Enfield identifies 'main' and 'specific' priorities for the service's three year plan (1990–93). These priorities shape the work of the LEA and the development planning of schools and colleges. The main priorities are:

1. Evaluation and Planning. Sound planning evaluation and review practices are regarded as central to an effective development process.

2. Organisation and resource management. Cooperative approaches to the management of schools are one of the implications of the ERA. Each school will need to extend its frameworks for planning and decision making to cover governing bodies and their sub committees, senior management teams and teaching and support staff. For the framework to be effective, roles, and responsibilities need to be clarified and made explicit, existing networks of communications and consultation reviewed, and policies drawn up within which the school will operate. The LEA and schools will need to plan for the monitoring and evaluation of LMS. Staff

and management development will be a priority during the period.

3. Partnership. More extensive implementation of cooperative working is an increasing priority.

4. Curriculum and assessment. Priorities for improvement include whole school assessment, curriculum planning and a broad and balanced curriculum for 16–19 year olds. It is intended to prepare LEA statements on teaching and learning, assessment, evaluation and equal opportunities.

Specific priorities include:

– equal opportunities where development is expected to embrace multi-cultural education, gender, and special needs;

– national and Enfield curriculum policy, schools are expected in their development planning to specify policies for the whole curiculum and cross curricular planning, language work and its role in learning, 16–19, information technology, design and technology, humanities especially the links between history and geography, pupil assessment within a whole school assessment policy and including records of achievement;

– appraisal for professional development, schools are advised to prepare schemes of staff appraisal.

The curriculum debate in Enfield

At the centre of the new management of education in Enfield is a preoccupation with developing the quality of teaching and learning. For much of the 1980s teachers joined officers and advisers in a review and redefinition of the curriculum. It began in 1981/82 when the Secondary Adviser took a group away for a residential course at Danbury Park to prepare the authority's first curriculum statement. This led to the Curriculum Initiative Group (CIG) and a number of studies over time including the ll–14 curriculum, TVEI, institutional development plans, and personal and social education.

we'd stumbled on a very creative way of working. We added to that group officers and advisers, people from further education, the deputy chief youth officer and so on, so that we had a very fertile group that became the Curriculum Initiatives Group. . . That model of development . . . worked very well and it was a little different from normal working parties . . . because you gradually developed a feeling that you left your status off at the door and simply became one of a group and it attracted a lot of radical spirits who really wanted to change things. . . So, that was a very exciting period for CIG, a period full of tension as well. But that collaborative approach, the feeling that there is a place where you can draw ideas from different parts of the system, different levels of the system, is very important. . . The whole is greater than the sum of all the parts. That if you create the right kind of mix of people, with enough space to do things, then what you actually get is a generation of energy and motivation which is actually much greater and things get done.

(the Chief Adviser, quoted from an MEd Thesis)

Heads began to learn that they gained extra resources when they won grants from this group for pilot projects. In 1985 a complementary Primary Initiatives Group was established to work with a number of schools on the development of the whole school curriculum. These groups, an adviser commented, reflected a new world: working in collaboration, the LEA providing 'seed corn' funding, and heads coming in to make the contract. The initiative groups illustrate the emergent Enfield culture of collective learning through discussion enabling consensus around central values of curriculum and the learning process. What had begun in 1982 as a response to a specific task turned into a creative way of working:

There was inevitably a professional emphasis in the earlier stages with considerable importance accorded to the process of involving teachers in the design of the curriculum. Following ERA, the challenge ahead for curriculum development will be to work more closely with parents and the community:

> When planning the curriculum, schools will have to take into account the particular combination of needs within the community. It will be important to involve parents in the education of their children even more closely than in the past because the authority believes that pupils learn best when their parents take on a direct role in the education of their children.

To this end, the three year plan from 1991 identifies the key priority of building the partnership with parents (while strategic planning has begun more systematically to enable parts of the service to set out their aims and accountabilities as their client groups would express them).

The Enfield framework for curriculum design involves clarifying the purposes and values of education that will shape the curriculum (understood as the way in which education is organised and made available to pupils). Enfield follow the Warnock Report in their definition of the purposes of education:

> Firstly, to enlarge a child's knowledge, experience and imaginative understanding, and thus his/her awareness of moral values and capacity for enjoyment; and secondly, to enable him/her to enter the world

after formal education is over as an active participant in society and a responsible contributor to it.

The core value is that the child lies at the centre of the learning process. Thus the design of the curriculum seeks to promote the values of equality of opportunity, a multi cultural education for all, and to ensure that those with special needs have the benefit of a full curriculum.

The aims of the curriculum follow HMI's well known *The Curriculum 5–16* but the LEA seeks to enrich them with a number of their own aims which emphasise the variety of learning, understanding of the world and one's contribution to it, developing self-confidence but also the ability to collaborate with others and to contribute to their well-being. Such aims express the active and social aims of the curriculum.

Planning for the curriculum as for development of the service in general sets the context for programmes of staff development and training, appraisal and evaluation schemes.

Flexible approaches to learning

A changing world and the demands it is placing upon individuals is causing the service radically to reappraise what people need to learn and how they should go about it. The capacity to be flexible and responsive to changing circumstances has encouraged the development of a new approach to teaching and learning in the authority. Education is most effective, it is believed, when students are allowed through flexible approaches to take an active and responsible role in their own learning.

> Learning how to learn is as important as what is learnt. It is a skill which has life long application and validity and which enhances opportunities for later education and training.
> Learning must allow the pupil to link new skills, knowledge, abilities and concepts to those he or she already possesses. It follows that teachers need to be aware of the point which each child has reached in his or her learning, and be certain that the recording and reviewing methods employed are capable of tracking each child's progress. Children learn more effectively when they are motivated by a sense of purpose and direction in their learning so that, as far as practicable, they should be aware of why and how, as well as what, they are learning, and also involved in the decisions being made about their learning programmes. The way this is done will, of course, depend upon the nature and age of the child.

The term *flexible resource based learning* is used to highlight the key elements of active learning – its flexibility, and the learner's interaction with a variety of resources, whether they are people, systems, books, or the environment. This perspective on learning is appropriate to any age group and is seen as the condition for providing the opportunities, encouraged in the LEA's curriculum statement, for students to:

- learn actively and gain first hand experience;
- explore, discover and solve problems;
- learn through discussion and debate;
- design, make and evaluate;
- gain experience of independent learning and develop study skills;
- work effectively in groups as well as individually;
- use a wide range of resources such as books, documents, audio-visual material, laboratory and workshop material, and flexible learning materials;
- meet the challenge of completing assignments, ranging from short exercises to more substantial projects, including cooperative ones;
- take responsibility for organising their learning experiences;
- consider and appraise their own work and progress and to set goals for further improvement;
- record their experiences and achievements and build up a record of achievement;
- create, express, enact, recount, and communicate with others using a variety of media;
- produce work for a variety of audiences;
- learn from adults in the wider community;
- use modern technology as an appropriate aid to learning and solving problems.

Flexible approaches to learning, it is argued, are central to the provision of these opportunities. A policy definition proposes:

Flexible resource based learning encourages active learning. The teacher acts as a facilitator and a resource for the student and aims to develop an environment in which students understand their responsibilities in the learning process and develop investigative research skills. Teachers remain responsible for learning by giving structure to learners' work and providing stimuli and resources. The students' learning experiences become more participatory and experiencial. Participatory learning involves the acquisition of skills which include the ability to communicate, investigate, organise, initiate, innovate. These lead to an empathy for and understanding of the subject matter. A flexible resource based learning strategy may be one of a range of classroom approaches. It is likely to be most effective when it arises in response to an agreed and identified learning need.

In this way teachers can respond sensitively to the individual learning needs of each child. At the same time teachers are encouraged to understand the contribution which families and others outside the school can make to children's learning (though also being alert to the external factors which place constraints upon effective learning. The objectives of flexible learning are supported by the systems of LMS and of planning and evaluation.

Local management of schools (LMS)

Enfield retains 16.5 per cent of the general schools budget for discretionary exceptions and hopes to reduce this proportion to 14 per cent over the next three years and will review further areas for delegation: such as repairs and maintenance, assistance to pupils and the tuition service, and other services to pupils with special needs.

For Enfield the new local management of schools provides an opportunity to develop strategies which support the authority's policies of partnership between neighbouring institutions. The management task is firstly to develop effective local management of schools and colleges through delegated financial management and the partnership scheme:

- providing adequate staffing resources to coordinate the preparation of schemes;
- involving teachers, officers, advisers and other staff as appropriate in the development of schemes;
- assessing the training needs related to local financial management (LFM) and school and college management for officers, teachers and governors and related staff;
- developing an information technology network to facilitate local financial management;
- developing revised financial regulations, staffing policies and guidelines and administrative guidelines in accordance with the provision of ERA, DES circulars and regulations;
- revising the instruments and articles of government for colleges and for school;
- planning for the implementation of schemes including the identification of the resource implications for the institutions and the education department.

Secondly, to develop an effective partnership between schools and between schools and the education department in order to help schools to respond to change and to improve the quality of education by assisting staff to cope with the pressure of rapid change through mutual support and informal consultancy; securing progression from one phase of education to another; sharing expertise, knowledge and skills; lightening the workload by sharing common tasks; developing revised financial regulations, staffing policies, and guidelines and administrative guidelines in accordance with the provisions of the ERA, circulars and regulations.

Supporting school evaluation and planning

Enfield has over a number of years developed a distinctive approach to school evaluation and planning whereby the schools together with the LEA pursue an integrated and collaborative approach. 'The approach in Enfield is based on the application of the principles of learning to all parts of the service whether it is the work of pupils, teachers, schools or the LEA itself'. The components of an improving learning quality are as follows.

(i) Partnership
Coherence, continuity, communication and shared goals are the conditions for school improvement. Turning partnership into practice means enabling teachers to come together within and across schools by creating and supporting networks for professional staff and curriculum development. Together with the partnership groups, the LEA has encouraged the formation of teacher groups, the teachers' centre, and curriculum working parties. 'Enfield has extensively used its collaboration networks to develop new ideas. A feature of the 1990s will be to use them to support all forms of evaluation, eg peer activity. In this way the support capacity of the education department can be combined with the schools and teachers on an organisational network to improve quality.

(ii) Evaluation
'Evaluation is not solely about the evaluation *of* schools but about using it as an improvement process *within*'. The Enfield approach involves the belief that the principles of learning are central to evaluation and planning and the work of teachers, schools, and the LEA. By this means pupil learning can become effective, schools are responsible alongside the LEA for ensuring the quality of education. Ultimately, schools should take the lead in assuring the quality of their work; the procedures and arrangements for

evaluation should build up the confidence, skills and practices of schools and staff from within. The intention is that this will create a professionally rigorous and open approach that combines the need to account to pupils and their parents as well as the general public; and the development process incorporates review and monitoring and leads to a strengthening of both. There are 'regular reviews', 'specific reviews', Borough wide surveys, and a five year review.

Evaluation policy in Enfield is based on a belief that the most effective outcomes from inspection are achieved when the school and the LEA have a shared role in the practice of monitoring and review and that the activity leads to enhanced quality in the school, together with an increased capacity to manage review and development. Therefore the LEA will provide an external perspective as an integral part of the process of school self-review. (Evaluation policy has been further codified in 1991.)

(iii) Planning
Enfield introduced school development planning in 1984. Institutional development plans (IDPs) incorporate evaluation which enables schools and the LEA to reconcile each other's development needs with those of the Government and individual teachers. Preparation of IDPs are informed by a statement of the LEA's priorities which are circulated to schools in what is known locally as 'the gold letter'. The review and planning process is an annual cycle which is being progressively interlinked with council, Government and other procedures.

Further education

The status given to the LEA, in the Education Reform Act to plan post-16 education has been welcomed by Enfield. This strategic role of the LEA is particularly emphasised in further education which in Enfield provides the framework for development planning in post compulsory education and training as a whole, incorporating developments in the technical and vocational education initiative (TVEI), the youth training scheme and employment training.

The LEA produces an annual plan in the context of a rolling three year plan using the model developed with the Manpower Services Commission in the planning of work related non-advanced further education and extended by some LEAs to the whole of NAFE:

This planning process must cover the whole of post-16 provision and is a very powerful tool for the LEA to use in meeting 'more effectively the changing needs of the population of the authority's area'. As the planning process is intended to ensure quality, cost-effectiveness and rationalisation, as well as regional coordination, it must form the basis of the LEAs role.

In September 1989 an annual programme for further education was prepared based upon the three year development plan (1989–1992) setting out specific objectives to maintain and, if at all possible, increase the responsiveness of FE provision to meet the needs of its customers (students and employers) within the community at large and to expand provision so that it is possible to provide for all who could benefit from it. This will include sections of the community not traditionally catered for by further education, particularly the unemployed and those with special needs; and to maintain existing levels of enrolment in the face of demographic decline, eg falling rolls and increasing competition from public and private sectors. The principal priorities for the annual programme, often prompted by the 1988 Education Reform Act, were to:

1. improve planning mechanisms across the post-16 sector, including adult and continuing education; a post-16 policy unit was established to develop a coherent policy for the sector, and the planning process became more formalised in the colleges;
2. improve resource and management information systems to support the planning process and the identification of needs: developing labour market intelligence on employment trends, skills shortages and skill changes; to develop a comprehensive marketing strategy based on detailed surveys of the needs of employers and potential students; to move towards formula based budget allocation and to improve systems of financial information and control, and to improve management monitoring and evaluation;
3. implement course evaluation by course teams;
4. implement flexible learning across the whole range of provision in order to make it more accessible;
5. increase the level of self-financing short course activity.

The annual programme also contained targets in developing a map of the curriculum together with the rationalisation of key programme areas; improving guidance and support; for equal opportunities policies in gender, ethnic monitoring, special needs and multi-cultural education.

Now, the three year plan (1991–1994) redefines and updates its strategies to take the service forward into the nineties. Partnership has become the founding value in support of the authority's central purpose 'to give all people living, working and studying in Enfield appropriate opportunities through education and training to develop their potential as individuals and as active and responsible members of society at work, at home and in relation to the community and the economy'. Equality, quality and flexibility express the key principles for the service to enable access and progression. The new target activities include:

- to map out a borough wide network of accredited programmes known and easily accessible to all potential clients;
- to take positive action where necessary to remove barriers and ensure equality of access and progression for clients who are vulnerable to discrimination on grounds of race, gender, special needs and child care responsibilities;
- to establish mechanisms for the assessment of prior learning and the planning, profiling and recording of personal achievement;
- to continue the strategy for phased implementation of the entitlement curriculum for full time courses by 1993;
- to continue to develop competence-based modularised courses, linked where possible to NVQs, together with the management, administration and staff development strategies needed to support the changes;
- to consolidate and take forward the use of flexible learning strategies as a major teaching and learning strategy for all curriculum delivery;
- to develop a strategy for the implementation and review of the borough's 16–19 education and training curriculum and policy statement;
- to expand and improve the use of work experience and workplace assessment across the FE service through new initiatives and partnerships forged by the Education Industry Centre.

As this last point implies, Enfield has made collaborative working with employers a priority and accordingly developed 'the Enfield Business Partnership' as the principal activity of the new Centre. The Partnership aims 'to raise the aspirations and achievements of young people and to allow them to maximise their potential in order for them to become part of a skilled and adaptable workforce'. The partnership involves twinning between schools and companies; the participation of employers in the curriculum and school and college management as tutors, consultants and governors; work experience and work shadowing for students and staff; and the exchange of services, expertise and facilities. The benefits which have been experienced include an enriched curriculum; more interested and motivated students; improved understanding of the world of work; staff development; and closer links with and support from the community.

Enfield is also taking the lead in the sub-regional planning of vocational education and training by bringing together a number of LEAs and colleges in North London so that local planning can be set in a wider context that will strengthen their collective strategic role. A project was set up to develop 'a metropolitan area model' for sub-regional further education strategic planning. Reports were produced in the autumn of 1989 and the spring of 1990. A number of strategic issues were perceived as priorities for sub-regional planning:

- planning and delivery exploring common themes and values in, for example, developing access and progression across the sub-region; coordinating specialist provision and preventing destructive competition;
- building an information base looking together at sub-regional information on labour market trends;
- developing the FE service working collectively to build partnerships with TECs; promoting public awareness of FE through collaborative marketing strategies and preparing together for the single European market.

The project worked through a consultative workshop approach which the participants believed would lead to a number of benefits:

that sub-regional liaison was not well established and that people needed to meet, talk and build a degree of mutual trust and understanding as a basis for cooperative action; that any sub-regional mechanisms would have to be fully owned by the participating colleges and LEAs, since it was clear that nothing other than the motivation of mutual interest would keep them in place.

Much progress has been achieved in realising these objectives and the project led to a Sub-Regional Strategic Planning Working Group which agreed 'that the current environment of FE requires a flexible approach to boundaries, whatever the untidiness of such an approach'. Its initial activities have focused upon joint marketing strategies, the development of TECs, issues of access and progression, and the single European market. The new three year plan concludes thus:

Flexibility and pluralism of approach will develop within agreed boundaries of partnership, strategic coherence and management controls. The central outcome will be a curriculum which seeks to maximise individual access, choice and achievement, and to promote the levels of skill, enterprise and opportunity which will empower the community to meet the challenges of the 1990s.

PART 2 1990–91 AND THE IMPACT OF CUTS

For the financial year 1991–92 Enfield Borough Council needed to prepare a budget which cut expenditure. The full effects of inflation during the year meant that the authority was entering the budget cycle for 1991–92 with substantial increases in expenditure unless cuts were made. The council wished to avoid being capped and this meant (because of the capping rules about 'high' percentage increases in expenditure year on year as well as levels of expenditure) that Enfield would be required to set expenditure levels virtually at the Government's standard spending assessments (SSAs). Nevertheless, even having persuaded Whitehall to set more reasonable SSAs, cuts were required. The councillors believed that anything was preferable to being capped having looked at its effects upon other London authorities. 'Anything was preferable to that'. So the primary task for the budget exercise, as perceived by the authority, was simply to find the cuts.

The Director of Education, however, sought to protect his service and the programme of reforms: 'from November 1990 till March 1991, I was involved in a very difficult exercise of trying to reduce our spending without doing too much damage'. Each service in the authority was asked to draw up a list of items to achieve a 2 per cent cut in controllable expenditure. Later, it was announced that any inescapable growth would have to be compensated for by cuts elsewhere in the budget. For Education this meant 'our 2 per cent shot up to 4 per cent and £4.3 million because there is a lot of inevitable growth flowing mainly from the Education Reform Act but also from other developments, for example in health and safety, which you have just got to find the money for'. For a time 'it did look until very late on as if we were going to lose anything from 120 to 200 teaching posts and it did look as if the whole service was liable and likely to disintegrate because of the enforced, rigid, cuts.'

The Director managed to persuade members that education, especially the general schools budget (and thus in delegated schools budgets), ought to receive priority in being protected from the worst effects of the cuts. This has meant in the end 'that the actual reductions in expenditure will be very modest in a full year (£100,000) although this disguises the fact that we have had to cut some things out (£2m) in order to put fresh things in and to pay for essential growth'.

The cuts included: instrumental tuition, the primary swimming programme, and nine posts in the Department's establishment (which the Director would have liked to use to enable the Department to develop its new functions). Particularly painful cuts had to be made to a number of budget items which provided essential resources to underpin activities that were regarded as strategic for the development of the service. These included what was called 'the initiatives budget' which supported the curriculum and other initiatives groups by paying for the release of teachers' time from their school work; designated secondments for people to gain approved qualifications but also to carry out work and research that would benefit the service; money for schools to release teachers to engage in their partnership activities; and money for in-service training that was not included in GEST ('we put a lot of our own money into INSET on top of Government grants').

A major crisis (cutting up to 200 teaching posts) has been averted but the remaining reductions could still nevertheless threaten those activities which were at the heart of the LEA's work to reform the service. Cutting 'time for curriculum development, time for the partnership, time for in-service training would potentially destroy everything that made for Enfield as a local education authority'. Although teachers have been saved time LEA wide development has been temporarily damaged: 'if schools have been stripped of resources then they have no capacity left to work together, to reflect upon or take part in Borough policies . . . it is wholly unrealistic to expect them to take part in the finer partnership networks that we are talking about'.

Yet although the cuts may have created short term damage to the partnership programme, they have provoked committed schools and teachers to defend it: 'it has enlivened those who feel strongly about partnership to come out and say so and, daft as it may seem it is for once reassuring to get anguished letters from headteachers saying we value partnership, you have actually destroyed our capacity for working together, we want it to continue, and what are you going to do next'. The Curriculum Initiatives Group, for example, are trying to find ways of continuing without the previous level of funding.

The Director and his Chief Adviser will, by September 1991, have reviewed the budget to identify resources ('every scrap of cash') which can be restored to support the partnership. 'So we won't have lost by this exercise, we will have actually gained because when things are going well the only messages you get are from the cynics or those who find difficulties easier to talk about than opportunities and you get a distorted picture. But once you do something which suggests that partnership is under real attack then a very large number of people are saying you are damaging something we value a great deal. . . So I think that some of the reservations about the partnership which I have mentioned in the past may have been too gloomy, because what you find in a crisis is that the roots are far deeper than you had imagined and people are more attached to partnership . . . you know there is nothing like a sight of the grave to make people appreciate life basically.'

The value of partnership has been revealed in the budgetary process itself, for the council's prioritising of education followed from the LEA's commitment to an open dialogue with members, governors and parents and to share with them the problems facing the service. For two years there has been a regular process of consultation with partnership groups with senior officers and members meeting the heads and chairs of governors. The financial position would be discussed and their priorities identified. Over time this has allowed 'a much greater consensus about what they saw as important and you have now got a coherent and united system behind the members of the Education Committee, particularly the Chairman'.

> It gives you much greater strength when you are speaking with conviction of knowing that what you are asking for is shared across the system and that's an essential part of the partnership scheme.
>
> It was our intention to get behind the formal system because we could see the danger that we would have a series of recommendations from governing bodies which the council couldn't meet, so that what could have built up was disappointed expectations and the only way you could get through that is to engage in discussions and to share the problems from the beginning with governors and parents and to show them that the Chairmen and myself were wrestling with the whole issue of insufficient funds. I think it has been a healthy dialogue, although I am not sure we have got everybody to take full advantage of the opportunities that are offered, but it has meant that for two years running now we have gone into a budget process very confident about what the schools feel is important.

It has armed the Chair in the Group and Policy Committee: 'it goes back to the art of warfare really, very clear, very clear objectives, concentrated forces and strike hard'.

Reviewing the education department

In 1990 a paper was prepared proposing that a review be under-taken of the department in the light of the 1988 Education Reform

Act. The department has a familiar pattern organisation including: a schools division, a further education division, an education personnel unit, finance and premises, a planing and review division and the advisory service. The report concluded 'that the department did not require a major reorganisation to fit it for its new role under the ERA, but changes were necessary to ensure it carried out its tasks effectively.' The schools and colleges divisions would review the levels of service required by institutions, schools sections would be modified to link with partnership support teams or partnership groups, while advisers and officers would recognise their triple role – support, evaluation and planning.

Nevertheless, by the autumn of 1990 the cycle of budgeting would lead to a number of posts (9/10) being taken out of the departmental establishment and by the early summer of 1991, the Director was reflecting upon the need to reorganise the department in order to reflect growing experience of managing the service following the ERA reforms. Once a service becomes oriented to the 'needs of the customer', it begins to face the dilemma of who its customer is. Different sections of the same Department are occasionally drawn into conflict in representing the claims of 'their' customer over, for example, admissions or complaints: one section reflecting the claims of parents while another reflects the claims of schools. This tension may reflect one of the new roles of the LEA to represent and adjudicate between interests of partners to the service. One part of the department would specialise in representing clients while another represented institutions. The reason for such a change would be that 'LMS places power with the institution and power is intolerant with oddities, isolating, punishing and excluding them (staff as well as pupils). Children with special needs and the minority communities may need even more protection in future. In the past the LEA would have moderated in the situation. But who now is to champion the claims and rights of clients. Should the LEA act as advocate for them. This needs to be thought through in organisational terms'. A review and adaptation of the department is expected.

The partnership approach to opting out

The development of a partnership perspective within Enfield is reaping benefits in relation to the threat of opting out as well as expenditure contraction. So far (June 1991), only one school has got as far as the first meeting of the governing body on opting out where the governors decided not to proceed (in the knowledge that the staff were overwhelmingly against). Cooperation rather than competition is the dominant force. 'The forces here are not competitive ones. The teachers as a group are quite clear that they would like to continue with the local authority, and the bulk of the secondary headteachers do seem positive about working within a local authority framework as long as the authority is determined to give them as much delegation, both of money and power, as possible, which is what we are about. That would enable them to cooperate freely from a very firm basis.'

Yet the LEA ackowledges that the balance of interest could change. 'What will force the teachers to change their minds, and they will do it, I think, as a group consultation with us, is if the rewards of opting out become so great that they cannot ignore them. And the rewards are tilting it that way already... The other thing that they will be forced to consider is the shortage of capital expenditure. The constraints on local authorities in terms of their capital spending are now so great that we are faced with a series of claims from schools for work which we know is essential but there is no hope of doing it all within the time scale they require. Somebody is bound to be tempted to think that if they were getting their funding direct from the DES, provided they had opted out they would get a more favourable treatment because we know that the GM schools, we have been informed so far, have been given a much greater share of the national capital allocation than their numbers would justify'.

Nevertheless, true to its defining values, the LEA did not wish to coerce its partners but to discuss the issues openly and fully. 'I think that the view which the secondary heads were taking collectively, with the Chairman and myself, was that we wanted to look at this very carefully (we wanted them to do this as a group and with others) and if they judged that the point had come when there were major advantages to schools by achieving grant maintained status, they believe they would want to do it as a group if possible, and in cooperation with the local authority, so that it would not be seen as a flight from the LEA, but as the inevitable consequence of different policy.' One school for whom it is very advantageous to opt out does not want to change its relationship with the school, and 'is deliberately holding back in order not to break the collective group of headteachers ... he and his governing body are quite conscious of what they are doing.'

One or two heads, it was pointed out however, would not subscribe to such a collective policy. One of whom is recently appointed. 'One of the things which is quite clear now (through sharing information across London) is that of the many reasons that schools start opting out one of them is because they have recently appointed headteachers – who have not put down their roots, who don't subscribe to the LEA and who are most tempted. They subscribe to all the values and systems when they join, but they haven't been there long enough to feel a real commitment to the local authority as a whole. . . You have to keep coming back to individual cases where schools might be tempted at particular points and you would have to look at it.'

The Enfield perspective on opting out, therefore, is that the authority and its schools should approach the subject as a rational issue examining the pros and cons. Whereas the first chair of Education following the Education Reform Act 'was fiercely against grant maintained status', the new chair takes a more neutral view and 'in reasonable circumstances would be willing to sell services to the school'. It could be the case that for schools the balance of advantage will tip decisively in favour of opting out 'in which case Enfield has developed a partnership scheme which will be used to sustain schools in a different kind of environment, and that was the original purpose of putting the network in there to make sure that if we disappeared schools would come to support each other'.

Learning between centre and locality

However rationally the LEA might approach the prospect of a collective opt out it responds, nevertheless, with alarm at the prospect for curriculum and educational development of the potential elimination of local government in education.

There is, of course, an important place for the centre. 'It is important, if you are trying to learn all the time, you have got to expose yourself to as many outside influences as possible. We have always given credit to national developments: to the Further Education Unit and A Basis for Choice was an important component in our earlier curriculum thinking; TVEI; the HMI's areas of experience, and the DES policy document on science was very good. . . So we have made use of everything we could, but we have kicked against some of the rigidities of the assumptions in the National Curriculum of a subject rather than a whole curriculum focus. . . Certainly if it hadn't been for the LEA's insistence on those aspects of the curriculum that run through the different subject areas then those would, I think, have been forgotten. The DES is now happy to accept that themes such as inter-personal relationships and social health education exist, but there is a danger that without the local authority's experience they could have been forgotten. . . Given everything we do leads us to collaborative models of learning and development we are bound not to be able to accept a model which says everything you can do is dictated from the centre: we simply could not live with such a model.'

It is not to say that the National Curriculum doesn't have a place as a framework, but as a broad framework. But it is because you need a notion of constant evolutionary development of the curriculum and of education you then also need to have local curriculum development. There is a blind spot at the moment and I can't see how we could carry on through the middle of the nineties without actually regenerating local curriculum development.

To be effective the curriculum has to be renewed to meet new local needs but also because teachers and schools have to believe in what they are doing if they are to be successful, and thus to take the glossy documents and tackle the difficult task of thinking it through themselves, to make sense of it. . . Individuals, schools and authorities have to think afresh about problems rather than accept a single orthodoxy. . . No one has a monopoly of the right approach . . . and it is important that the school or the authority continues to assert its individuality and the fact of difference because otherwise you switch in educational terms to an authoritarian state. The larger the system the greater the capacity for being wrong on a larger scale.

Local curriculum development has to come back again. After all one of the reasons why GCSE was implemented so effectively was because a lot of local curriculum development had taken place prior to its construction, a lot of things had happened beforehand. Similarly with the National Curriculum in science: it came in on the back of all the changes which had been going on in science education locally. So I think that the success of any National Curriculum depends upon the capital of local curriculum development.

The model of change is mistaken. It must not be the mere implementation of something external to us but rather as harnessing the National Curriculum requirements within the learning model which we are developing. Neither inspection reports nor National Curriculum documents alone can cause change. Rather it is the pressure which derives from a local authority with a community of professionals working collaboratively across the system with members to develop education.

No government could carry out reforms of the educational system without a local body interested in seeing the best bits of those reforms developed. If there is nothing between the DES and the school you will build in inertia.

Conclusion

Enfield's distinctive response to the 1988 reforms has been to understand that semi-autonomous institutions can only flourish within a context of mutual cooperation which continues to require the strategic leadership and support of the LEA. Consortia of schools alone would be insufficient to the provision of learning quality. The principle of partnership is the LEA's key to the new management of education. The role of the LEA is to develop the conditions for such collaborative working to emerge, and in Enfield this has meant an emphasis upon adaptable networks which enable the partners to create shared values and policies.

At the centre of the new management in Enfield is a preoccupation with curriculum development and the quality of teaching and learning. Education is most effective it is argued when pupils and students are encouraged through a flexible approach to learning, to take an active and responsible role in their own learning programmes.

The principle of learning, indeed, underpins the whole management of education in Enfield – an openness to new ideas and a commitment to reflect upon and integrate the experience of others in order to improve understanding of good practice. The approach has been 'to work from complexity to simplicity', to support a number of small scale projects developing different aspects or models of a policy issue – whether it be appraisal, or records of achievement, or school review – and then develop a deeper more secure shared understanding of what the best practice for the LEA should be. 'Records of achievement would be an example where a number of different approaches have been tried through which we have been able to simplify the essence of good practice, so that you end with a Borough approach to which everybody feels they have contributed. . . Groups discuss the principles to a point where they become thoroughly embedded in their understanding and they become your advocates.'

The key to managing change in Enfield has involved the creative interrelating of:

(a) leadership with a clear vision of education, the future management of the service, and a commitment to a distinctive style and process of managing by encouraging participative and collaborative working; particularly significant is the management of key political relationships and the relationships of mutual trust established with the chair and the committee;

(b) an enabling LEA, committed to devolving responsibility to partnership groups but also to strategic planning that will provide a firm framework both for their flexible networking and for schools to develop their own thinking;

(c) an imaginatively led network of teachers, advisors and officers committed to exploring and sharing excellent practice in curriculum development and flexible learning; 'dotted around

the whole authority are lots of different developments supported by initiative groups (by initiatives money and grants
money), as well as working groups and the teachers' committee', this network creates the environment, builds the
interdependence for the learning LEA:

> You need what I think is a firm framework of principles and then that
> quite complex network of groups all contributing to different aspects
> of those principles: without the framework the groups wouldn't have
> anything to attach to; without the network the principles would be
> empty – I suppose it's like trying to grow something on a trellis, or
> vines

(d) the involvement of teachers in 'initiative groups' so that
change, rather than being top down, emerges from the
reflective practice of teachers and lecturers as well as officers
and advisers;

(e) a strong teachers' centre promoting the best in professional
and management development in schools.

The management of change in Enfield embodies a model of
learning: 'In order to take in all the changes, nationally and
locally, and improve the quality of what's going on, all the change
processes must incorporate opportunities for learning either by the
child, the teacher, or the school, and for us as an authority. You have
got to have the . . . means and the arrangements therefore, because
learning doesn't take place in isolation, of supporting people in their
learning. That is why the networks outside and between schools are
so important, because you don't always learn as effectively when
trapped within your own context, you need to step outside a bit,
or be helped from outside to reflect upon what you are doing'.

4
Kent County Council
For service to the customer

PART 1 FROM 1988

Understanding the direction of change

The education service in Kent County Council has like the other LEAs in this study developed a very clear understanding of the context in which it is working and the trends of change that have to be managed with new skills and qualities:

> The world of education is undergoing rapid and unprecedented change. New legislation will transform the role of local authorities in education. It is of paramount importance for Kent County Council to manage this change positively if we are to continue to provide the best possible education service for our pupils and students. The education department will need to change in order to manage change.

The major influences are perceived as: the 1988 Education Reform Act which introduces greater accountability and responsiveness to *customers* by delegating management responsibility to governors; the 1988 Local Government Act, which introduces competitive tendering for a number of local authority services; and the policy initiatives of Kent County Council in devolving management responsibility throughout the authority.

These influences, it is believed, 'will fundamentally change the education system as we know it. Power will move from the centre – County Hall and Springfield – to schools and colleges. We cannot resist this change, nor should we. The County Council is determined to devolve management responsibility close to points of delivery'. Putting the customer first (and the major customer is the institution) will require a change of culture in the service.

Such changes in relationships between the LEA and its institutions will need each part of the service to understand their new roles and management tasks. 'In future we will need to lead, persuade and influence schools to implement the County Council's policies and objectives. The days of telling schools what to do are gone. We will place a premium on the leadership, negotiating and marketing skills of senior managers. The essential skills will include: management of change, policy development, customer care, leadership, negotiation, marketing and performance review.'

Education service mission statement

The purpose of the education service in Kent is to provide and enhance the quality of the educational experience gained by its pupils and students, thereby helping them to achieve their maximum potential and meeting their continuing needs and the changing needs of the community at large. It should be the aim of everyone working in the education service in Kent to be able to relate his or her activities to that purpose. To achieve this the values of customer service have been established as the new mission of Kent County Council. 'The big difference between Kent and many other LEAs is that we are now committed to a change of culture which puts the customer first. This means that in everything we do we must ask what will the benefits be for the customer. The questions we need to ask ourselves individually and collectively are:

- Who are the customers for our services?
- What do they require from us?
- What do they have to say about the services we provide?
- How can we improve the services in the light of this?
- How can we make the service more accessible and available?'

Certain principles should be applied in carrying out the job of providing an education service:

- a commitment to openness in dealing with the customers of our services;
- a willingness to listen and provide accurate and adequate information so that a basis for trust is established;
- giving staff the responsibility for that part of the service which they provide;
- the setting of high standards and doing the very best we can, at the same time being very self-critical; willing to admit error and to learn from it.

The education service exists to provide support to schools and colleges and others directly involved in the delivery of education services. Since all are involved in the delivery of these services for the people of Kent, all are needed to work together; teamwork is therefore a special priority. This means:

- having clear statements of policy;
- much less bureaucracy;
- more active management;
- more responsibility and accountability throughout the service;
- greater participation in policy-making;
- increased responsiveness;
- much better communication with the public;
- more effective cooperation with our customers and other staff.

In interpreting and implementing this mission statement, the education service will adopt an open, innovative, sensitive and dynamic style of management.

The management principles of the department

A distinctive approach to management is being developed that is appropriate to the values of service to the customer. The management principles are:

- Getting closer to the customer means changing the focus of attention to the sharp end of the organisation where the relationship with our various customers takes place.
- Devolution involves clarifying individual responsibilities and then holding managers accountable for their performance. Importantly, it means giving managers control over the resources necessary to do their job.
- Developing an approach which is managerial rather than administrative means we need trained managers who see themselves as accountable for the management and performance of their part of the organisation.

These principles embody the management philosophy expressed in *In Search of Excellence* (Peters and Waterman, 1981). That is, a commitment to management as a process which celebrates and practices a culture of quality as service to the customer. The characteristics of excellent companies in the private sector are, it can be argued, as appropriate to the public sector: a value-driven organisation, 'close to the customer', strategic leadership, decentralised discretion in implementation, valuing staff, giving staff their head and encouraging innovation, and simpler organisational forms.

This is a modern style of management which, it is believed, can make education more efficient and effective in responding to the needs of its customers. This perspective has coincided with the arrival of the new chief education officer. In a *Times Educational Supplement* commentary it was reported: 'these developments represent a new breed of aggressive management which is beginning to sweep county halls and education departments around the country. The CEO represents a new breed of officer: more managerial and less professional. This does not mean he is less interested in the curriculum, but, he claims, the days of gifted amateurism are over'.

Local management of schools

Kent has approached local management of schools with enthusiasm because it embodies the authority's principles for managing education. 'We anticipated the Education Reform Act through our piloting of LMS.' Local management will, it is firmly asserted, improve the effectiveness of school management: 'The Kent scheme for the local management of schools is more than a series of budget and accounting procedures. It is part of a process to enable headteachers and governors to manage schools effectively and efficiently by providing the information and support they need to make management decisions and giving them the freedom to determine the use of resources to meet the needs and priorities they have identified. Local management of schools is a new form of partnership between the LEA and schools.'

Kent is delegating more of its budget and to more schools than most other LEAs. In its scheme Kent says that 'the authority has decided to include all schools in the local management scheme. It wants to do this as quickly as possible, and is looking at ways of enabling schools to take on some LM-type responsibilities in advance of entering the actual scheme, in particular as all schools will be operating on formula budgets from April 1990, whether or not they are in the LM scheme'.

In April 1990 87 of the schools in Kent's pilot scheme of local management transferred to the Education Reform Act scheme, and will be joined by a further 133 schools. It was planned originally that by April 1991 there would be an extension to 277 other schools, mainly schools with over 200 pupils on roll, and the intention was to include the remaining smaller primary schools, special schools and the nursery schools, 270 schools in all, in April 1992. In 1991, however, it was decided 'to go the whole hog': 'all primary and secondary schools are fully into local management from April 1991 – certainly the largest LM scheme in the country'.

The formula allocates over 80 per cent of delegated expenditure by age weighted pupil units. This is used to allocate most of the costs, though some special factors include a lump sum to protect the curriculum at small primary schools, a split site school factor, and a salary protection factor for small primary schools are distributed through other mechanisms. The formula also eases the transition to prevent large budget changes.

The role of the LEA in the new ERA

The new customer oriented management of education will require a revision of the role and function of the LEA. 'If we are going to respond to what schools want, this means that we are over a good period of time going to have to clear out from the management role of the Authority a lot of the routine administrative work and we are going to put into the hands of the schools the money and the discretion to buy services.' The new role of the LEA is, it is claimed, quite straightforward: to devise strategy, to produce the budget that will make possible the delivery of strategy, quality assurance and, where necessary, to support institutions.

The department perceived the Audit Commission report (1989) on the *Losing an Empire, Finding a Role: The LEA of the Future* as reflecting many of the changes in the management of education which they had already embarked upon. The new roles would include:

- leadership in articulating the vision of the service;
- devising strategy, plans and budgets;
- support schools, colleges and other educational establishments; in this way the relationship between the LEA and its institutions will increasingly become that of a 'club';

The mechanisms for advice and support to schools will also need to change. Traditionally, it has mainly been through the advisory service to teachers. In the future, the scope of advice and support will need to be enlarged, the diagnosis of educational problems must go deeper and the destination of advice and support will be more directed at heads, principals and particularly governing bodies.

- a banker, channelling the funds which enable local institutions to deliver;
- a regulator of quality, monitoring and evaluating performance in schools and colleges;

Kent like the Audit Commission, sees the LEA effectively acting 'as the "agent" for its ultimate customers by procuring education and training for them through a range of institutions. Increasingly, in continuing education and training at least, that is how the LEA will need to operate. There may be other sectors to which the principle applies also. This role, it is argued, will have considerable implications for the way in which the LEA fulfils its quality assurance function. For instance reports on institutions and services will need to be expressed in a form which addresses the concerns of non-experts. This will mean a more structured approach to inspections than previously and the results converted into publicly available information on performance.'

– a provider of information to the education market, helping parents and the public to make informed choices between types of educational institution and on the basis of judgements about performance.

There will be a clear distinction between the role of the centre and area offices. The centre will concentrate on strategic county-wide matters and provide policy direction. Responsibilities will include: strategic management of the service; policy development; provision of specialist leadership and advice; and county-wide monitoring and review known as quality assurance.

It is believed to be particularly important for an authority as large as Kent to maintain consistent standards and ensure that services reflect the policies of the County Council. Headquarters would have a major role in this respect.

– Day-to-day matters will be separated from policy and review to establish a clear focus for the latter.
– The Centre will have a departmental 'head of profession' relationship with area offices for a number of activites such as finance, personnel and other services like careers and the psychological service.
– The education department will acquire a stronger 'client role' in relation to its land and property.
– FE colleges will be able to receive any day-to-day management support they need from area offices rather than the centre.

As area offices become the contact point for all schools and colleges, direct and support services to education establishments will be devolved from the centre to the areas. The plan for the area offices differs from the existing situation in four major respects:

1. All staff based in the areas will be responsible to the Area Director. Specialists in the area offices will, however, retain a relationship with their departmental 'head of profession' at the centre.
   This implies a major reshaping of accountabilities and affects area-based staff in the inspectorate, careers service and school

psychological service who currently report directly to the centre,

2. The plan is intended to broaden substantially the management responsibilities of the Area Directors,
3. A 'practice accounts' system will become operational throughout the department. In essence this means delegating the budget for support services to schools and giving them the freedom to 'buy' such services from area offices, other County Council departments or, ultimately, the private sector,
4. A higher profile is proposed for services to customers, and in particular higher level advice should be made available to governors to reflect the increased importance of governing bodies. As part of this exercise an extensive governor training programme has been introduced.

Priorities for the management of change

The education department has responded to the context of reform with a number of changes to its organisation and management. It is clear however that a further programme of change will be needed to ensure that the department is ready for the new management of education:

- *Culture* – demonstration of customer service and recognition of difference by the public; evidence that education rather than administration is paramount; establish a relaxed but brisk management style.
- *Policy* – a clear officer focus for assisting members in developing strategic policies.
- *Resource management* – there is scope for further budgetary devolution and for the budget and management structures to be aligned; finance under control and used creatively.
- *Monitoring/review* – local management will require a much more comprehensive approach to the monitoring of school performance in terms of both education and management performance.
- *Organisational development* – areas self-standing and confident, but integrated.
- *Staff development* – interchange of staff between areas, areas and the centre, and education and other departments.
- *Accountabilities* – there should be a clear distinction of responsibilities between the centre and the area offices. Lines of accountability should be simplified throughout the department.
- *Information systems* there is a need for better information

systems to give managers easy access to data essential to the control of devolved budgets. A more business-oriented approach to the funding, development and operation of information systems is required.
- *Training* – the existing investment of £250,000 in non-teaching training in the education department needs to be further extended into key areas such as budget management and information systems; in addition customer
 awareness; organisational development, and personnel issues.
- *Kent's profile* – raised nationally and positively.

Such priorities, agreed with leading elected members, were designed to enable the department to adopt its role to the full and were formulated in targets for the development of the various services.

The review of secondary schools

Perhaps the most challenging issue of managing change for Kent has been the need to review its provision of school places in the context of falling rolls. Given the authority's commitment to local management of schools, to parental choice and to a plurality of secondary systems any rationalisation of secondary provision would be a particularly difficult undertaking. In January 1990 a report reviewed the viability of secondary provision in the county. The report indicated the substantial fall in pupil numbers during the 1980s without any prospect of recovery during the 1990s requires a significant reduction in the number of school places:

> By the early 1990s there will be about one quarter fewer pupils (30,000) in secondary schools than the peak reached in 1980. The effect is not evenly spread and while some schools are still full and under pressure others have suffered greater than 25 per cent loss of pupils. This makes the provision of good education difficult and expensive. Declining schools have needed extra finance in order to retain teaching staff to cover the curriculum. In addition there are large revenue costs: to achieve the DES target of removing 3 in 5 of the surplus places in secondary schools (19,000) would save £3.8m on premises' running costs. Money would be better spent on improving provision in schools which are strong and have an assured future.
> Analysis of the intake to secondary schools in September 1989 shows a large number will soon be below the size considered the minimum . . .
> The schools which are falling below the size considered capable of providing a satisfactory curriculum are of all types: high, grammar, wide-ability and middle schools . . .
> The combined effects of falling pupil numbers, the requirement to provide a broad and balanced (national) curriculum and the funding of schools on the local management formula can be anticipated with

certainty. Schools which are not strong, ie of sufficient size and quality, will go to the wall. The choice for the LEA is either to let this happen naturally but painfully, or to manage the situation.

The conclusion advocated the latter course of action: 'there is no way that a significant restructuring of secondary education in Kent can be avoided . . . it gives an unprecedented challenge and opportunity to reshape the county's secondary education to meet the demands of the future'. The LEA proposed to respond to the challenge by: rationalising the age of transfer to eleven plus; promulgating guidelines on the viable size of a school; and approving a package of school closure and amalgamation. New arrangements would be determined for the conduct of public consultation meetings. The reorganisation of school places would prevent the waste of resources which were needed to respond to the development of curriculum and assessment.

The Kent curriculum statement

This document sets out policies on the curriculum and teaching approaches for children aged 5–16 in the county. It is designed to provide guidance for schools 'in this era of great educational change and opportunity'. Much of the material in the statement was generated by discussions following the publication of the consultation document in 1988. In defining and constructing the curriculum, areas of learning and experience together with subject areas have been chosen to match the National Curriculum, but 'schools are expected to review the curriculum each year, using the statement as a bench mark and taking account of their own special circumstances'. Like other LEAs, Kent adopts HMI's educational aims, but with interesting variations:

- to maintain and develop in pupils lively inquiring minds, to promote the ability to question and argue rationally, to encourage pupils to apply themselves to a range of tasks and skills;
- to emphasise the importance of language, number, the aesthetic and physical areas of learning and to develop competence in them;
- to foster attitudes which will instil self-confidence in pupils, create in them a sense of personal excellence and help them to acquire knowledge and skills relevant to life in a fast changing world;
- to help children develop perceptive, spiritual and moral values, and an understanding of the beliefs of others;

- to help pupils understand the world in which they live and the interdependence of individuals, groups and nations;
- to develop in pupils the ability to appreciate critically human achievements and aspirations.

These aims are pursued through the curriculum which is understood, following HMI, as 'all those activities designed or encouraged within a school's organisational framework to promote the intellectual, personal, social and physical development of its pupils'. The foundations of the curriculum include the National Curriculum together with cross curricular areas of learning and experience. The curriculum, moreover, should be characterised by breadth, balance, relevance, differentiation, progression, continuity and coherence.

Kent 'expects its schools to promote equality of opportunity for all pupils' and to develop a range of successful teaching strategies towards achieving these goals. Each school is required to have an agreed statement on equality of opportunity that is understood as 'a fundamental aspect of the ethos of every school and is thus the responsibility of all involved in a school'. A coherent and powerful set of rights to equal opportunities are set out. Pupils have a right:

- not to be devalued on grounds of accent or language, home circumstances, ethnic origin . . . gender or disability; . . . this is essential for the healthy self-image and thus the motivation of all pupils;
- to feel one's heritage is understood and appreciated, together with the values one brings to school: as maturity develops, the right to be supported in negotiating an identity for oneself which integrates the qualities of home and school;
- to a learning environment, including curriculum and resources, which dispels ignorance, prejudice and stereotyping: pastorally the right to protection from insults, abuse and bullying;
- to a sense of social justice and community in the classroom and school, leading to a shared awareness of the duties and responsibilities of individuals, and to a perception of the interdependence of the community and the wider society.

To achieve these ends, schools have identifed a range of successful strategies of teaching and learning:

- encouraging and consolidating parental involvement in all aspects of school activity;
- affirming the pupil centred approach, by developing the linguistic and cultural resources that the child brings to school, and integrating them into the learning process;

- openness in promoting investigative and collaborative modes of teaching and learning, so that all can participate and fulfil their potential;
- realising the opportunities provided within all activites for incorporating a variety of perspectives;
- recognising that each subject area, and its delivery, can be enhanced by a dimension which affirms equal opportunities and cultural diversity;
- establishing an ethos, by means of a whole school policy, which protects individuals from prejudice and discrimination both overt and covert.

Education is expected to prepare pupils for life in the wider community, and help to develop the concepts, skills, attitudes and ways of behaving which are appropriate to promoting good relationships and eradicating ignorance and prejudice in a pluralist society. Pupils need to be supported in developing an understanding and appreciation of each other's culture, and in recognising and overcoming bias and discrimination.

Schools are also encouraged to develop a partnership with industry and the community. 'Whilst providing all young people with a broad economic awareness, a partnership will enable pupils to gain an understanding of the changing industrial/technological nature of society, and of their place within that society. A partnership will also enable pupils to develop an understanding of the opportunities and expectations within the world of work.'

Having developed the curriculum and the process of learning, procedures are necessary to monitor and evaluate their effect in schools and colleges. Kent has given particular emphasis to quality assurance in the new management of education.

Quality assurance

Kent perceives that within the Education Reform Act quality assurance becomes the means by which fulfilment of statutory duties and achievement of policy objectives are tested and reviewed. Following the Education Reform Act, the LEA believed that it was 'pioneering a completely new approach to monitoring and improving service delivery'.

> Kent is seeking to develop a total quality programme which pervades the whole organisation. It is about the way people at all levels do their job. The improvement of quality is not a technique but an attitude which comes from people who care and show commitment (this is why it is called a quality assurance (QA) rather than a quality

control programme). The Kent QA programme is comprehensive and involves all functions of the education service. It requires identification of outcomes of delivery and gives responsibility to the Head of Quality Assurance to scrutinize any aspect of the education service in Kent. This process, including the development of appropriate performance indicators, is already influencing levels of service delivery in educational establishments, in the education department itself, and is affecting the development of educational policy. Any quality assurance programme, particularly in a climate of local management, must cover all aspects of the service which are relevant to efficiency, effectiveness and economy. Monitoring and evaluating the authority's education provision must happen continuously through the process of self-review, survey review and inspection. The majority of this information will be published within the public domain. Kent has deliberately chosen the term quality assurance rather than quality control and is determined that it is recognised as being the responsibility of all managers, heads of establishments, governors and members. The challenge is to provide a picture of the quality of service but the outcomes of that process must also be supportive to the service.

Quality assurance 'monitoring standards of service and performance everywhere', therefore, was to form a new approach that is the key to the new management of education in Kent. The new approach would comprise:

- more formal and frequent inspections which will be related to self-evaluation by schools;
- a more comprehensive approach to the monitoring of performance involving collation of information on managerial and administrative efficiency and effectiveness, as well as on teaching practice;
- the application of quality assurance in LEA offices as well as in schools and colleges;
- the development of performance indicators for all parts of the service;
- flexibility – in future inspection and reviews will be undertaken by a wide range of specialists drawn from the education inspectorate but also including officers with financial, personnel, IS and managerial expertise;
- quality assurance will become an integral part of management, consequently, it will be the manager's job in the first instance to collect basic information on the performance of his or her unit.

This programme of performance review was, in the LEA's own estimation, 'ambitious'. The aim was to carry out a routine evaluation of every institution at least twice a year to complement the institution's own annual self-review. In addition each area team would seek to achieve a cycle of reviews of its institutions, supported by at least one area full inspection per year. County surveys would be programmed annually to monitor primary, secondary, further, youth and community, and adult education. It is proposed that reports for both area and full inspections would be published from April 1990 and available for a wider audience than hitherto. Such reports would, in the first instance, be considered by governing bodies and in due course the appropriate education sub-committee.

It was recognised that a condition for the success of such a quality assurance programme would be a reliable data base of information about school, colleges and other institutions. 'The ability to retrieve from evidence across a broad spectrum of relevant activities and process it into a succinct and readable presentation will be a fundamental element of the quality assurance programme.'

Planning of further education

A process of strategic planning lay at the centre of Kent's scheme of delegation for further and higher education in the county. Plans for the sector would be based upon the preparation of a three year medium term plan, reviewed and rolled forward annually. An annual programme of provision would be drawn up each year linked closely to, and part of, the budget planning process, setting out projected student numbers in broadly based subject areas.

The LEA believes the strategy should embrace the whole post-16 field, identifying the range of provision for which the LEA is responsible and to define the respective roles of the secondary and further education sectors in securing provision. The plan should take into account the private provision of education as well as continuing education offered by community schools and colleges, voluntary bodies and university extra mural departments.

The overall plan should include the work related FE plan and the contracted programme with the Training Agency (as it then was). The strategic plan should be integrated with and seek to influence LEA policies for manpower and financial planning.

Six area 16–19 coordinating committees would be responsible for coordinating the plans and provision of FHE colleges and 16–19 provision in schools. The TVEI consortia would play the leading role in curriculum coordination and planning: every school in Kent is a member of a consortium and every consortium includes the local colleges in its membership. The planning process should reflect analysis of need and be based upon extensive consultation with the colleges. Factors to be taken into account in post-16 planning include:

- projected student demand, including demographic trends;
- developments in new forms of provision and learning methods;
- value for money, using performance indicators and management information;
- special needs provision and those with learning difficulties;
- labour market intelligence.

Participation and consultation should play a central role in planning. 'The involvement of colleges in planning procedures will take place at all stages, for it is intended that the FHE plans should be owned by colleges and the LEA as a corporate entity. Joint consultations would focus on the college development plans, which would form an essential part of the three year FHE (rolling) plan, and the annual plan.'

It was hoped that the scheme of delegation for further education in Kent would provide colleges with considerable freedom to manage their affairs within the authority's overall strategic framework, and that it would create the conditions for the increased responsiveness of college management to the changing needs of students, employers and the local community.

Reorganisation of the education department

Kent reviewed its management structure in 1987–88 and determined it had a very fragmented structure, 'in effect there were a number of different services, and there was a gap between policy and operational accountability'. There was not a lot of disagreement about the kind of structure which was needed, one which was committed to devolution, LMS and 'to getting accountability out to the areas'. This meant devolving support services to the areas, including advisers, finance, personnel support, building maintenance, adult education and the youth service. The role of the centre would be strategy and quality assurance (the whole of quality, including, for example, financial and information support).

At the end of 1988, a new management structure was agreed for the education department. The Director of Education is supported by three principal branches to the department: 'strategy', 'quality assurance' and 'operations' with (indirect) responsibility for the area offices. Appointments were made to these positions on five year contracts. 'Head of profession' arrangements were established for the education department in relationship to the area offices for a number of activities such as finance, personnel, careers and the psychological service.

An evolutionary approach to reorganisation was established that involved identifying the 'management superstructure' first and following it with proposals for detailed staffing structures later. The management structure at the centre provided an opportunity to fuse theory and practice through the 'practice accounts' mechanism. For example it is anticipated that the head of strategy would use the expertise of the FE inspectors in the curriculum review team in order to draw up NAFE plans for colleges. Similarly, the head of operations would need the expertise of the finance team to monitor area offices' expenditure against their budgets whilst the head of quality assurance will use the finance team to assess on an annual basis the performance of area office finance teams. Budgets are being devised with practice accounts in mind and charging systems are being introduced.

In the area structure, finance and personnel professionals report directly to the area director. The customer services section provides a wide range of pupil and student services and an integrated approach to special needs. School psychologists and careers staff report to the head of customer services rather than to the professional heads at HQ. Similar arrangements exist for the head of curriculum support (ie the senior area inspector) who reports to the area director rather than the chief inspector. The 12 national curriculum specialists with county-wide responsibilities are located in area offices rather than HQ. A major exercise of relocation took place between the centre and area offices with the transfer of many functions to the areas.

PART 2 1991 AND THE BUDGET CUTS

The new Director of Education had in his first year of office, secured a growth of £3 m in the education budget: he aimed to achieve growth of £12 m by 1998. In the context of such ambitious objectives the budget cycle through the winter of 1990, to prepare for the 1991/92 budget, was to prove a particularly painful exercise for the education service. Budget cuts of £9 m had to be found and at one stage a cut of £20 m was being contemplated. The largest budget heads had to bear the burden of financial reduction: the inspectorate and advisory service; careers service, youth and community, awards, and administration. A cuts exercise was undertaken in high secrecy in February 1991. The scale of cuts was bound to be damaging to the service. This can be illustrated by examining the implications for the quality assurance branch of the service which was, as indicated above, accorded such a key priority in the new management of education in Kent.

Quality assurance in retreat

The impact of the cuts upon the inspectorate and advisory service, and the high profile quality assurance programme was particularly traumatic: a £2 m reduction. In effect the service was cut by 50 per cent even though 60 per cent of the total budget is funded from national GEST grants (and thus only 40 per cent of the budget had to be found from County Council resources). The Chief Inspector had to identify 'something like 65 posts to be taken out of the old structure'. To ensure that as many senior staff as possible were retained the burden of redeployment fell upon the advisory teachers.

This level of reduction required a radical revision of the inspectorate and advisory service. A number of key principles about the purpose of the service were clarified:

- providing strategic advice to members, the director and the area directors;
- the need for county wide monitoring;
- the need for area support;
- the need to support subject developments such as the national curriculum

A number of models were produced and the one which emerged with the most support following widespread consultation and discussion was the one which protected the area structure as much as possible, because devolution was an intrinsic value, but also 'because the customers were telling us that that was what they wanted. But the size of the county, together with the budget constraints, indicated that a completely devolved service was not possible' and the pressures to centralise many of the services have been inescapable. So a structure with three components was devised, and implemented in April 1991:

1. To set up a central curriculum support unit (CSU) which would be based at Maidstone and service the whole county for secondary subject advice as well as for the cross curricular themes. The CSU would also house the assessment unit, together with the French project, the history centre and the small business project. With the exception of the assessment unit all had been based previously in the areas. A devolved structure was in effect being centralised.

   A formula has been devised to determine an entitlement, of roughly 10 person days, for each school. Schools would pay for support over and above their entitlement and schools in general are being encouraged to enter into an annual contract with the unit for advisory support. The market would determine the provision of advice so that if the demand was high for technology rather than say geography the unit would need to sell the time of the geographer to pay for employing more technology advisers.

The unit as a whole is to be given twelve months to become self-financing and until then to enter into contractual arrangements with as many organisations as possible, including grant maintained and independent sector schools, as well as county schools which have decided to buy advisory services over and above their entitlement.

2. To keep a structure at area level, but with much smaller teams focusing on the needs of primary schools. (In some areas the CSU may be perceived as a rival and in competition for the custom of the school in that area.)

3. Before the reorganisation, each of the areas had teachers centres which housed teams of advisory teachers. Now they are empty spaces to be used for courses and meetings – in one area it is known as 'a key under the mat centre'. In all areas the future of the centre is under threat because of the number of courses needed to make them viable.

4. To centralise the inspection and management review functions. Two small teams of inspectors (primary and secondary) are now based centrally at Springfield.

What all this implied was a wholesale revision of the inspection strategy. The routine inspections and reviews for every institution has had to give way to a light sampling approach determined by the centre rather than the area teams. Moreover, in the new structure the dual role of the old area inspectors – responsible both for pastoral support and evaluative reporting – comes to an end, with the roles being differentiated around specialist advisers in the areas and inspectors at the centre. The necessary integration of evaluation and advice is retained through the key line managers, the senior area inspectors and the chief inspector.

The area teams will be expected to 'get close to the schools' because their jobs, like the unit's, will be on the line. If GEST funding dries up then whether the advisers continue to be employed will depend upon whether they are wanted by schools.

The £2 m cuts have left their mark on the service. Revising the service was at first a demoralising experience: 'you looked into the depths and realised that you were going to savage a service that you had worked hard to build up'. Yet senior managers while recognising that the service will no longer be able to provide the services that it did before, ('you have to jettison some of those things which you perhaps ought to be doing anyway') have sought to look at some of the virtues of a very different model that has had to be implemented:

- eliminating the tension (between advice and inspection) in the role of the old pastoral inspector;
- having to set up many of the services as self-financing cost-centre businesses sooner rather than later, 'could very well be the salvation of the LEA, because the trend to opting out is starting to peel off the layers of the LEA. We are now in a position of being able to go out and sell services and get that money back in';
- returning to the classroom many of the advisory teachers who had been in the role too long.

The service has had to be 'shaken up, so that people realise they are working in a flexible manner now, that they have to be responsive to change and that they are as good as their last customer says they are. When you are in the market if you are not providing the service which members and the schools want then your job is no longer secure. So a lot of home truths have been uneasily appreciated'.

Nevertheless, in the last resort there is sadness at what has been lost. An external review of the service by Leicester University reported that the previous structure and its services were highly regarded by schools which now believe that someting of value has been lost. Schools, in particular, valued the institutional reviews and a team of inspectors coming into a school to review its progress and identify development needs.

> So, there are negatives . . . and while it is necessary to go out and promote the new model . . . we must not kid anyone that it is anything other than a different service. We can't do what we did before and staff must not give the impression that they can do all that they were doing before, or it will ruin their health. We must not give people the impression that we can make such swinging cuts without them having serious effects upon the service.

The budget cuts are interacting with other aspects of policy in the Education Reform Act.

LMS and school budgets

The climate of budget reductions together with the effect of the LMS formula creating 'losers' as well as 'winners' is having a damaging effect on the schools which are experiencing declining resources.

'There is a lot of evidence that some schools are able to provide better learning environments under LMS, painting rooms, laying down carpets, improved book supplies and resources for CDT. But in the poorer schools there is a general retrenchment. These schools are having to retreat to a sterile curriculum and money is not being spent on special needs. So policy is having the effect of creating a have and have not situation.' The budget contraction is also interacting with another aspect of Education Reform Act policy – that on opting out.

Opting out and the future of Kent as an LEA

The trend to opting out is accelerating faster in Kent than in any other LEA, and at a rate that will bring the future of the LEA into question. It is not certain whether the Department of Education and Science, let alone Kent County Council have come to terms with the consequences of most or all schools in an authority choosing to acquire grant maintained status: 'I think the DES are now in disarray on opting out, they can't cope and are nervous about the next wave of opting out'. Kent are now at a critical stage on opting out with the future of the LEA literally in the balance.

The position in the spring of 1991 was that four of Kent's 141 secondary schools had been given approval by the Secretary of State to opt out. The first, a girls' grammar school, became grant maintained in October 1989 and, in April 1991 the complementary boys' grammar school together with two Maidestone high schools became grant maintained. A further 11 schools have seriously embarked on the opting out route and are at various stages of obtaining approval. Two more schools were accepted by the Secretary of State and one rejected by him in July 1991. A number of other secondary schools have explored the possibility of opting out and some primary schools have considered the option although only one has proceeded to formal voting.

There have been a number of reasons which have precipitated the move to opting out in Kent. The first wave of applications has not in the main been motivated by financial reasons. When the legislation was first enacted schools benefitted only by a small start up grant, an increased chance of finance for building improvements and by receiving directly the cash equivalent of that proportion of the cost of running the school which the LEA had previously incurred. For Kent this last figure was comparatively low, less than 13 per cent of the general schools budget (to pay for provision of advisory services, school meals, administration of payroll, personnel, finance, curriculum support and other support services).

Yet the schools which have chosen to opt out have done so in the main in response to the LEA's policies on school reorganisation – either to avoid closure, or to avoid a change in the character of the school. Kent believes that the policies of the DES are likely to encourage more schools to seek grant maintained status:

> while opting out will continue to provide a way for schools to side step policies they do not welcome, it must be anticipated that a continuation of DES policies will encourage more schools, including some primary schools to opt out.

In October 1990, the Secretary of State had announced that all primary schools could now apply to become grant maintained; at the same time the one-off grants were increased; and the DES continues to favour grant maintained schools as far as capital programmes are concerned. Moreover, the DES' decision to grant all grant maintained school an annual sum of 16 per cent of an LEA's general schools budget is causing particular concern for Kent: 'it means that GM schools will get more than the cost of services they usually receive'.

> This has serious implications for us. The *extra* cost on the Kent County Council budget of the four already approved grant maintained schools and the eight which seemed destined to opt out would be well over £400,000 in 1991–92. Under present arrangements this would have to come off the budgets of other schools. For future years, it would mean either a reduction of service to the LEA schools or an extra cost to the community charge payer. Moreover it would put a question mark against the committee's policy of delegating further finance to schools. Representations have been made to the DES on this issue, proposing that the calculation of the grant should continue to be made on an actual rather than a notional basis.

The LEA would seek to adjust the non-delegated elements in the budget so that maintained schools in Kent were not disadvantaged. One concern about the process of approving grant maintained schools is the uncertainty it creates for budgetting 'when schools opt out during the year it makes it difficult for us to plan the budget'.

So although finance was not one of the primary reasons initially for opting out, it has increasingly become so. Schools are now opting out for a number of reasons:

> firstly because of the lack of basic funding. We have underfunded schools, and they are being squeezed here faster than elsewhere. One can understand when a head tells a colleague that he is now earning £40 k. (It's a nasty one that the head's salary bit!) Secondly, property and the state of maintenance. We need to spend £40 m desperately on some badly maintained schools. And thirdly, policy. We have a secondary school system in which, however much you say the high schools or the comprehensive schools are good, it is clear that Kent is only interested in grammar schools. The capital goes to them and there

is a bias in the revenue funding through an attempt to massage LMS.
So you can understand that 80 per cent of heads are disenchanted with
the local authority. There is an image of meanness and yet of plush (local
authority) offices and glossy brochures.
GMS is a Black and Decker drill in this context. It is a fallacy that you
can strip the parts without damaging the whole.

The consequences

The growing trend of opting out is having a number of effects:
upon competitions between schools; it is feared that there will
be consequences for particular communities, and for the authority
there are fatal financial consequences if the trend continues.

The competition between schools is intensifying as a result of the
trend to opting out as well as open enrolment; some might say that
the policies introduced in 1988 are now beginning to work. But with
some interesting twists. One officer spoke of the increasing trend to
competition between schools:

> Would Mr Baker have introduced LMS if he had realised that opted
> out schools would undermine the selective system as it has here in
> Kent. The high schools are opting out because the LEA is planning to
> eliminate 13+ selection: the aim of the LEA is to increase competition
> to enable all schools, on an equal LMS footing, to develop a distinctive
> ethos. The strategy is to enable grammar schools to admit below the 25
> ability band and to allow high schools to admit into the top ability band.
> Schools in effect will become more equal, less selective.
> The high schools think that this policy will benefit the grammar schools
> and cause them to lose their existing higher ability level 11–13 children
> who will be drawn to the grammar schools at 11+. They believe this will
> threaten their viability, their marketability, and are seeking to opt out to
> protect themselves.

Another officer believed that some high schools would survive in
the competitive market place, although the larger, well established
grammar schools would remain:

> The high schools are going grant maintained to compete with the
> grammar schools and we anticipate them 'seeing off' the weaker
> grammar schools. The stronger ones will remain unaffected.
> On the other hand two small grammar schools have been allowed to
> opt out and they are now extending their boundaries and the spread
> of their admissions to ensure survival.
> Other grammar schools are seeing opting out as a kind of return to the
> old direct grant status.

Opting out, some feel, is an opting out of the public service
which will have serious consequences for particular communities

and for society generally. Whereas LEA maintained schools have responsibilities to serve, and be a resource for, the community as a whole, this is not the case with GM schools which are under no obligation to provide equal access to the public.

There will be a backlash in effect upon the community. There will be serious problems for society if the needs of the community as a whole, especially those with special needs, are not provided for. The vote in one London Borough was for 'not wanting council children'. When schools become separate, individual islands they will damage the communities as communities. If sink schools emerge, as they will, this will damage a sector of the community, it will damage the economy, and it will damage individuals. We are sheltering a social disaster if we undermine the public service and public education.

The portending of collapse of public education is, it seems, no mere rhetoric in Kent. The LEA is especially concerned about the serious financial consequences of the emerging scale of opting out:

Setting out the GMS problem: the Kent case

The likely position in Kent by 1993 is 60 per cent of secondaries opted out and 10 per cent of primaries opted out. In educational terms this is acceptable if strong schools opt out, but the indications are that the weak schools are being allowed to opt out and will therefore lower the average quality of education.

1. At the present rate, a substantial proportion of the GM schools would otherwise have been closed because of falling numbers (as a result of parental choice) leaving about 20 schools more than we need: that is, we are unable to remove surplus places:

    This will produce an inefficiency cost of £4m + per annum

2. We shall only be able to allow market forces to operate (ie withering on the vine) with the educational damage to existing pupils in dying schools:

    This will produce high educational damage

3. An incoherent system will exist with high schools becoming comprehensive schools by stealth, threatening the grammar schools, and the grammar schools will broaden their intake to say 40 per cent which effectively changes their nature:

    This will produce lower educational standards

4. There will be hindrance to an improved vocational balance for 14 to 18 year olds because, for at least the first few years, grant maintained schools will give priority to proving their academic pedigree:

    This will produce inappropriate education

Cont'd

---

5. The proliferation of uneconomic and narrow sixth forms will syphon finance from maintained schools:

   This will produce poor educational experience

6. The continuation of schools on an unplanned basis means that some will be in the wrong place while local schools close:

   This will produce extra transport costs

7. The LEA will be left with a rump of secondary schools requiring above-average unit cost when we are trying to delegate more finance:

   This will produce policy which is inconsistent

8. The introduction from 1 April 1991 of the statutory 16 per cent proportion of general schools budget to grant maintained schools will cause Kent to halt and even reverse the process of delegation of finance to schools:

   The DES needs to decide which policy is priority

9. The concentration of 'problem pupils', be it behavioural or learning problems, into the rump of schools counteracting the accepted value of integration:

   This will produce higher unit cost and exacerbate the cycle of deprivation.

In practice the policy is damaging LEAs which the Government favours while leaving others untouched. We have lean administration, low management costs, maximum delegation, advanced local management, unrivalled choice of schools for parents and yet more schools are leaving Kent LEA. (One school has opted out in Liverpool, none in Manchester, none are seeking opting out in Lambeth or Hackney, but four are in Wandsworth and 13 are in Kent.)

The policy is hitting the wrong target: an urgent, fundamental rethink is needed

At a time when the UK needs stronger and more efficient education with improved standards and better response to economic demands there is rapidly diminishing capacity to plan.

The incoherence will be economically, financially, educationally and socially damaging.

Figure 1

while we are succeeding in establishing local management effectively and will continue towards 'fully-fledged' local management in response to the wishes of schools, it is necessary now to consider how the strength of the LEA's services to schools can be sustained despite the syphoning off of substantial funds by the DES to be paid direct to grant maintained schools. The fact that the LEA would lose more than £2 m if all 15 schools were to opt out concentrates our thinking.

The LEA, it is claimed, might survive 10 per cent of schools opting out, but 20 per cent will destroy it. Thirty GM schools would cost £5.6 m out of the budget, 'and we would be on the edge of bankruptcy'.

Emerging policy towards opting out

There is some disenchantment amongst officers and members that an authority like Kent which has committed itself to the principle of LMS is actually being penalised: 'we are paying for going quickly into LMS whereas some northern LEAs have held back on LMS, little has changed and they will be less damaged by the 16 per cent regulation.'

It is the view of the LEA that allowing schools to opt out of the LEA is not a sound policy for the development of an efficient and effective education system. The pressures to seek grant maintained status are recognised: school reorganisation plans and the threat of closure; a change of character, or shortage of finance and capital. Moreover, the whole climate of recent years is one which encourages individual school interest diminishing concern for the wider community. Yet it remains the responsibility of the LEA to plan the provision of education in as effective and beneficial way as possible; beneficial, that is, both to the pupils and to the people of Kent who meet many of the costs of education. The legislation on opting out makes it difficult, the LEA argues, for the authority to exercise these responsibilities. The incidence of opting out together with the decision-making of the Secretary of State raise doubts about the wisdom for the LEA of proposing schemes of school reorganisation, amalgamation or closure to remove surplus places and improve the efficiency and effectiveness of educational provision. 'It does seem that the Secretary of State's criteria for approving schools to opt out are less stringent than anticipated and that unless the school is in an exceptionally weak position..it will receive approval to opt out if it chooses to take that route in order to avoid closure. This is in direct conflict with previous DES advice and Audit Commission exhortations to take surplus places out of use'.

Kent believe that their experience reveals an uncertainty and lack of planning nationally about the consequences of widespread opting out. A further reorganisation of the management of education nationally would be necessary unless the Government is content to accept unplanned and incoherent development.

The LEA consider that the context had changed considerably and that a review of the authority's policies towards opting out was necessary. It was realistic now for the LEA to anticipate at least a steady stream of opt out applications with a worst case scenario of 60 per cent of secondary schools and 10 per cent of primary schools achieving grant maintained status by 1993. The LEA believed that such an outcome would have major implications for policy and finance.

Such drastic financial implications have caused the LEA to alter its stance towards opted out schools. Whereas the initial orientation of the authority was to refuse to provide services for grant maintained schools, now it is clearly in the financial interests of the LEA to contract to sell services to opted out schools. 'While those schools remaining with the LEA must continue to have priority and we shall maintain our drive to provide services of a quality which makes it attractive for them to stay with the LEA, it is necessary for us to relate to schools which are considering opting out in such a way that they will wish to continue to use our services. In due course it will lead to services being offered to independent schools as well as grant maintained schools and to schools in other LEAs.'

Thus Kent, having been opposed to opting out, is now taking a neutral stance towards GM schools. The LEA would not only market a series of services to GM schools (including payroll, personnel, finance, curriculum, inspection and advice, information about county developments, information about primary links and so on) the authority would also encourage them to take out 'associate status' with the county.

The government white papers and the reorganisation of post-16 education

Kent welcomed the overall aims of the reforms to engage more young people in education and training and to improve their attainment levels. Many of the more detailed objectives are also regarded as valuable: promoting the equal status for academic and vocational qualifications, improving vocational progression routes in schools, extending training credits, and improving the information and guidance offered to students. Indeed, the LEA believes that many of the proposals are similar to their own recent Review of Work Related Education and Training (WRET). Nevertheless, it is believed that the White Papers create many problems for LEAs and the planning of effective provision for young people:

> In particular, the proposals arbitrarily divide post-16 provision between school sixth forms on the one hand and FE and sixth form colleges on the other, thus making it dificult to achieve consistence, coherence, and the 'tertiary approach' recommended by the WRET review. This

problem is likely to be exacerbated since the White Paper goes to some lengths to reduce the role of the LEAs in the new arrangements to an absolute minumum.

It is also a matter of regret that there is little or no recognition of the work LEAs have done successfully towards the aims set out in the White Paper, for example in developing close education/employer links, developing the Technical and Vocational Education Initiative, supporting the new Training and Enterprise Councils, increasing staying on rates in colleges, introducing the National Curriculum, GCSE, and making the major contribution to the substantial involvement of the education and training system over the last decade, which the White Paper recognises.

The new funding council involves a major shift of power from LEAs to central Government and for the authority 'it is a matter of concern that there is no provision for LEA representation on the funding council or, more particularly, its regional advisory committees, although the latter will include TEC representation. Similarly, whilst the regional advisory committees will be asked to take account of TECs in fulfilling their functions, there is no such requirement to consult LEAs'.

The authority is concerned about the lack of clarity and potential confusion in planning for the 16 to 18 age group as a whole. In future, LEAs will only retain a power (as opposed to a duty) to provide sixth form places, while the strategic duty to provide sufficient full time education for all in this age group transfers to the new councils. But their responsibilities in relation to school sixth form provision remains unclear. 'It would be helpful if the Government were to clarify its intentions on such issues as whether the funding of sixth form provision by LEAs would continue unaffected or be subject to some form of control; whether the funding council would be able to support sixth form provision directly; and whether the council would have powers to close sixth forms.' Kent believes that consistency and coherence suggest that it would make sense for the council to take over the planning and funding of sixth forms.

The LEA concludes its analysis of the implications of the White Paper by commending the laudable aims of many of the Government's proposals which 'echo many of the recommendations of Kent's WRET review and it will benefit the young people of Kent if the White Paper can meet its aims of producing more access to and greater comparability betwen different forms of post-16 education and training'. However, there are significant reservations and concerns:

There can be little doubt that the separation of FE colleges from the remainder of Kent education service will make it more difficult, but no less important, to take forward the WRET initiatives, in particular the aim of securing an integrated tertiary approach to work related education and training. The separation of vocational and non-vocational courses is not helpful in improving access to continuing education for adults and ways have to be found to bridge the divide which could exist . . . (and)

it is a matter of concern and regret that the Government intended to achieve these aims through the central funding of FE and sixth form colleges, thus separating them from the remainder of the local education service and from clear local accountability and from the sources of local experiences which have moved education and training forward in recent years.

A place for local government in the future of education

The recent changes are, it is believed, creating an uncertainty which cannot be sustained, and a review of the governance of education is required with some urgency. The Director has a clear view about the framework of government and management of education that can provide the conditions for an education with entitlement and opportunity for all. The principles which would have to underlie any new structure are: first, the importance of retaining some local democratic accountability in the delivery of a service which needs to be essentially local in character; second, that the central and fundamental responsibility of the Education Acts 1944–1988 to provide education for every child can only be effectively discharged through a decision-making process which gives powers as well as duties to a local planning authority for education; and third, that high standards in teaching and learning will have to be secured, in part, by local inspection and local professional support.

A local structure, therefore, is needed to help secure a national education system of the highest quality, accessible to all and meeting their educational needs. It should enable the statutory tasks and provide the necessary support services so as to allow for the benefits of economies of scale. The significance of the local system would be such as to attract and retain excellent professional staff to offer the quality of service required by local people.

The purpose of the education system should be to provide entitlement and access for all, opportunities and challenge for parents and students, and high standards of teaching and learning. To enable these purposes, the primary functions of the local education authority should be:

- *Planning* determining democratically the pattern of educational provision in response to demography, local views,

and criteria of educational quality and cost effectiveness. The pattern of provision should maximise the continuity of education for individual students as they progress between primary, secondary and tertiary phases. Such planned provision is needed to complement free market initiatives;

- *Funding* determining the level of revenue funding for schools and colleges and the equitable distribution of resources between institutions in the light of local conditions; the level of capital investment in buildings; and the funding of locally-determined services which 'add-value' to the basic educational provision: for example, under 5s, community education, youth service, cultural, recreational and sporting opportunities;
- *Statutory duties* discharging a variety of statutory functions especially those directly relating to pupils and students, for example, special needs, transport, awards and benefits, child welfare and careers;
- *Quality assurance* securing for parents and students:

  - high standards of teaching and learning through local professional inspection, monitoring and support;
  - a high standard of education for all students whatever their personal circumstances and learning needs;
  - a wide range of relevant educational opportunities;
  - a court of appeal, arbitration or advice in cases of unresolved dispute, disagreement or confusion, that is independent of the institution.

  Providing for heads, principals and governors:

  - an external validation of standards of teaching and learning, and of managerial effectiveness.

  Acting as local manager for national schemes:

  - in supporting the effective implementation of educational and legislative developments: for example, GCSE, TVEI, schemes of local financial management, the National Curriculum, student assessment and teacher appraisal.

- *Support services* responding to a market-led demand for consultancy and support services, relating to: management, professional development, curriculum, finance, personnel and property, information, pastoral, and trouble shooting. Such functions are needed locally to serve the educational needs of individuals and the community. 'To avoid fragmentation and debilitation of the education system a decision on how the education service is to be managed will have to be made – and soon'.

Conclusion

Kent County Council is distinguished by its commitment to the new management of excellence which places service to the customer at the centre of its mission. Education will improve its performance in service delivery and in standards of achievement when it learns to respond more effectively to the expressed wishes of its customers – schools and colleges and, beyond, parents and employers.

The ambitions of the LEA included devolving more decision-making to encourage responsiveness and improved communication with schools and colleges, while the function of the department would focus increasingly upon providing managerial leadership through strategic planning and quality assurance. A major priority had been to develop a total quality programme which pervades the whole service combining internal review with external inspections to maximise accountability.

Senior managers of the service, however, have always been clear that the new system of education management which was being envisaged for the service required a number of conditions if it was to be effective. The idea of lean administration at the centre, with devolved authority and responsibilities to semi-autonomous institutions competing more equally, presupposed an efficient infra-structure of resources. Together with some continuity in local government finance, this required a plan to reorganise schools in order to remove surplus capacity and thus the waste of scarce resources. But this implies, for Kent as for some other counties, that they faced a considerable dilemma of needing to create the infrastructure for the new management through careful planning in an era which prefers free choice of the market.

5
Manchester City Council
For equality of opportunity

PART 1 FROM 1988

Manchester local authority has for a number of years been striving to support the regeneration of a City that has been suffering the effects of economic recession and restructuring. Central to this revival is the task of raising the aspirations and expectations of the young people of the City many of whom, especially the disadvantaged, have been underachieving. A distinctive strategy of educational renewal has focused upon the reform of teaching and learning, driven by values which commit the service in all its dimensions to policies of equality of opportunity and the benefits of working in partnership with parents and the community. The reforms of the Education Act are supported to the extent that they reinforce the Manchester agenda for change.

The authority believes that 'a full entitlement to education can only happen when due regard is paid to the local context'. While it is appropriate for statutory requirements to set out the nation's minimum expectations for each young person they, nevertheless, 'do not consider the educational or social environment within which these expectations are to be realised'. To neglect the context in which young people learn would be to limit their potential achievement. The LEA, therefore, has developed values and policies which reflect the needs of the local community and parents within the Manchester context.

That context is often one of disadvantage. One in three Mancunians are affected by degrees of poverty and this is more typically the experience of the ethnic minority communities whose rate of unemployment is more than one and a half times that for white people.

The material disadvantage and deprivation of working class children is also emphasised. '*Attainments are depressed, partly because of the low expectation of teachers and of parents, who must be more closely involved.* Language or cultural differences may inhibit communication and poverty is increased because benefits are not claimed, and access to educational advice may seem restricted.'

> The barriers of class discrimination continue to limit the opportunities to pupils, and must be recognised and overcome if pupils are to have the genuine equality of opportunity.

It is not that poverty, poor health and housing 'determine' the ability to learn, but 'much energy may be devoted to overcoming the difficulties with which they live'. The evidence suggests that where schools and the education service generally are sensitive to the context of learning then children make greater progress – increase their skills, confidence and capacity. Effective schools are better at fostering a climate for learning that is supported by parents, governors and teachers. Manchester has sought to develop policies and practices which support the service in providing opportunities for all young people to overcome any circumstance of disadvantage.

Principles to shape reform

Three interrelated key values and principles are shaping the programme of educational reform in Manchester:

1. Equality of opportunity in education
'Barriers to equal and fair treatment are most usually found in prejudices linked to power. The barriers can be seen from several perspectives all connected by the similar unjust effects on people's lives and life chances. People may be discriminated against in this way on account of their gender, racial, ethnic, social or class perspective, sexual orientation or disability. *In education full equal opportunities will only exist when the system is free from those discriminatory practices which impede the development of a large proportion of children and young people.*'

Providing the same programme of study ignores the influence of gender or ethnicity and the stereotyped expectations which often limit the development of children. Schools, therefore, have a duty to enable girls as well as boys to develop according to their capacities and hopes, while all cultures and ethnic backgrounds must be presented in positive images.

2. *The rights of parents*
Parents are the child's first educators. They have a right to be involved in their child's education by being informed of their development and having the opportunity to participate in school and classroom activities. The school will need to explain to parents what it is seeking to achieve, so that they can support the child's learning in the home. It is well accepted that children make better progress when parents and teachers work together and decisions are shared. This is a process where schools not only accept parents but give them support so that they can make their own contribution to their child's education. Parents should have more:

- information about their child's attainment;
- involvement in decisions about their child's educational future;
- involvement in school activities;
- support from people working with their child;
- support from other parents;
- respect and acceptance for their skills as parents;
- respect when differences of opinion occur;
- training and support for parent governors;
- opportunities to meet other parents.

Parents can be encouraged to participate as 'full complementary educators' by sharing their skills; engaging in school-community project work with pupils or in cooperative working in school; assessing achievement; working as a parent governor; participating in assemblies; helping with social events or running a parents group. The Chief Education Officer has called for a Bill of Rights for Parents to secure improved help and support, access to information, opportunities for participation and joint decision-making. 'The real involvement of parents in the education process will not only be a challenge but provide a major opportunity for breaking the circle of underfulfilled working class talent. Parental rights will enable the realisation of equality of educational opportunity. Rights can be secured through partnership.

3. *Partnership with home and community*
Education takes place in the home, neighbourhood and community as well as in school. Parents, governors and teachers, therefore, have to work together to develop effective schools. The school is an important part of the community in which it is situated and should seek at times to challenge, at others to reflect the attitudes and values of the community. Home, school and community are inter-related parts of a child's life and the relations of cooperation

and partnership between them are vital to the educational progress of young people. *The notion of partnership involves all school staff, parents, representatives of the community and the school governors. Each has a part to play in the development of the curriculum.* In a genuine partnership each member:

- shares the same central aim of developing the full education of the young person;
- maintains the integrity of each partner;
- recognises values and builds upon each role.

The Chief Education Officer has written that 'in a democracy it is essential that all partners in the education system share a commitment to the system which determines what is taught and how it is taught'.

The new government of local education

Manchester supports a number of the 1988 legislative reforms, 'not the political gimmicks such as the CTCs and opting out', but the idea of a new framework of management with the LEA focusing upon strategic leadership and quality. It is acknowledged that LEAs have not exercised sufficient leadership over local education in the last twenty five years, being too preoccupied with matters of building and administration to the neglect of the big questions of learning and achievement. Schools, moreover, should be given more delegated powers to manage teaching and learning to meet the needs of their particular children and communities. In Manchester, however, schools will not be autonomous institutions but working together within agreed plans developed collectively by the City.

> The education committee will set the framework within which governing bodies will exercise their delegated powers. The committee will articulate policies for the service, including its curriculum policy, and coordinate national and local specific grant initiatives. It will remain the owner of county school premises and its powers in relation to the organisation of schools will continue to be central to the planning of the service. The committee will retain statutory responsibility for the assessment of pupils with special educational needs and for ensuring that the needs of such pupils are met. It will continue to have the main responsibility for the professional development of its teachers, including appraisal and in-service training. The committee's monitoring and evaluation role will be of particular importance in ensuring that its

overall responsibility for the service is discharged in an effective and efficient manner.

The LEA will delegate powers under the local management of schools, but identifies the clear need for the education committee to retain control of certain discretionary exceptions that allow the authority to provide services which schools need if they are to be effective and meet the equal opportunity policies of the authority.

The powers and responsibilities of governing bodies are set out with an emphasis upon their accountability to the local education authority. Governors have the responsibility of implementing the National Curriculum taking into account the LEA's curriculum policy. They have the freedom to deploy resources within the school's budget to meet their own educational needs and so can determine the number and kind of staff to appoint (in the case of county schools, taking into account the advice of the chief education officer as well as the headteacher). It is for the governing body, in partnership with the head, to develop and carry forward a management plan for their school. The LEA understands that governors and headteachers may make managerial mistakes but, nevertheless, they are required to be answerable for them. The LEA's responsibility is to sustain and support governing bodies with information, professional guidance and appropriate training to ensure that governors have the appropriate skills to take on their duties.

The managerial role of headteachers is encouraged by the LEA which recognises that they are already managers and that they are now given powers to match their responsibilities. The education committee expects that across the whole range of decisions relating to local management the governing body will consult and take advice from the headteacher. The head will have a key role in helping the governing body to formulate a management plan for the school, and in securing its implementation with the collective support of the school's staff.

The new proactive LEA

Legislative change while taking away powers nevertheless creates opportunities for LEAs to 'develop proactive policies which can bring about real change and improve standards'. The most important of these opportunities are:

1. giving governing bodies as much advice and support as possible to allow them to take full responsibility for the management of their own institutions;

2.   providing leadership in all curriculum areas both with respect to content and methodology;
3.   working closely with the diocesan authorities in respect of planning provision, finance and support arrangements;
4.   working with parents – information about school/colleges, benefits, special educational needs, involvement in the process of education;
5.   actively involving young people/learners and other users of community education, particularly in the exercise of choice;
6.   providing specialist technical support, eg financial, legal, buildings, welfare, personnel function;
7.   involving employers in the process of policy development and implementation, eg post-16 colleges and Compact;
8.   involving local communities in decision-making processes, eg governing bodies, management committees;
9.   counselling, advice and publicity;
10. generating income;
11. allocating strategic revenue;
12. marketing, including labour market information;
13. developing evaluation of institutions.

These evolving functions would develop together with other LEA responsibilities: planning the system of places; strategic planning for post-16 education; determining policy and practice for special educational needs; budgeting; the management of employment; the provision of services (pre-five; youth and community); support and advise, monitoring and evaluating schools and colleges; responsibility for testing arrangements; staff and governor training; informing parents; enforcing school attendance and managing statutory exclusions function.

The possibility of providing strategic leadership for the service is perceived as compatible with a process of devolved management.

Local management of schools

The key to any success in the new management of education lies in partnership between the LEA, governors and teachers:

> The successful operation of this scheme for the local management of schools is dependent upon the continuation of the working partnership which has long existed between and among pupils and parents; school staff and headteachers; the local community; governors and Manchester Education Committee and their officers. That partnership is committed to working towards the agreed single underlying purpose of achieving

the maximum benefit for their children, by providing in Manchester schools the highest standard of education within a rich and happy experience of school life.

The scheme reflects City policy that a new pattern of management can improve the quality of education in schools. The LEA will 'devolve decision making to local/neighbourhood levels, through maximum delegation of financial and managerial responsibilities to governing bodies' consistent with the DES and the LEA discharging their responsibilities. Where it is more efficient to do so 'a limited number of services' will be provided centrally. Delegated management will be complemented by the education committee developing 'a strategic role having the lead function in a number of areas'; the resource availability, the scope of delegation and the basis for resource allocation, the conditions within which governing bodies must operate, monitoring school performance, and the operation of sanctions.

The formula should be intelligible to parents and the community as well as governors and teachers, and should assess the needs of schools on an objective rather than historic pattern of expenditure. The determinant of need will be pupil numbers but also the incidence of poverty and special educational needs. The LEA reserves the right to include 'minor variations from time to time to reflect changes in the composition of the schools budget' including decisions to improve pupil–teacher ratios, or to account for actual teacher rather than average teacher costs.

These form significant changes to the guidelines provided by the DES who have yet to approve Manchester's scheme. The LEA is convinced that unless there is more flexibility within the formula for allocating resources so as to protect deprived schools or schools which have (sometimes necessarily so) unusual staff profiles, then the prescribed guidelines will undermine an authority's commitment to equal educational opportunities.

Local management for equal opportunities

The new legislation, while defining the LEA as 'the employer', accords governors the power to appoint and dismiss staff. Manchester has, therefore, been concerned to ensure that governing bodies comply with the council's equal opportunities on employment. The education committee, therefore, have commended to governors the City council's policies which they believe represent an excellent basis upon which to develop equality of opportunity in all spheres of a school's activities. To this end a number of documents are provided for the information and guidance of governors, headteachers and others. They include:

1. A general statement of equal opportunities policies within the education service in Manchester.
2. Equal opportunities in employment: a policy statement by Manchester City Council. This includes a code of practice on recruitment and selection which is an integral part of their equal opportunities policies.
3. Workforce audit, including ethnic monitoring. An important tool in any effort to increase equality of opportunity in employment is the workforce audit. The City Council strongly supports the collection of data about ethnic origins, disability and gender and require the completion of a monitoring form by all persons newly appointed to posts within the council as a condition of their offer of employment.
4. Changing the composition of the workforce and the setting of global equality targets. The council is encouraged that the Government accepts the recommendations of the Swann Report (On the Education of Children from Ethnic Minority Groups) that steps should be taken to increase the proportion of teacher force drawn from the ethnic minority communities. It is also accepted that ethnic monitoring of the teacher force provides an essential back-up in implementing this policy.
   (Circular 8/89 from the DES requires each LEA to collect information about the ethnic origins of all its school teachers and to make an annual return to the Department. The DES supports the view that 'in the wider public sphere, the collection of ethnically-based data is becoming increasingly recognised as a means of identifying need and thus helping to ensure fair and equal treatment for all'.)

Local management for the community use of schools

The LEA encourages the maximum possible community use of school premises during evenings, weekends and school holidays for a wide range of educational, social and recreational activities. While the 1986 (no.2) Education Act requires governors to have regard to the desirability of premises being made available for community use, the City is more explicit in promoting the value of community participation:

> Existing support from schools for community activity is well established, and recognises that community education providers, including non-statutory groups have the right to use facilities outside normal hours, and that school premises belong to the community as a whole rather than exclusively to the staff and pupils of individual establishments.

School development planning

Drawing upon the DES report (1989), *Planning for School Development*, Manchester reinforces the significance of whole school development planning for improving the quality of learning and performance. Planning will enable schools to organise what they are already doing and what they need to do in a more purposeful and coherent way. Aims and values together with future priorities for action can be turned into a strategic plan which can be modified and changed over time. A pro-forma is completed by all schools in five sections:

1. Evaluate progress in relation to previous year's priorities.
2. Statement of agreed priorities for the forthcoming three years – at the levels of team, and department as well as the school. These priorities are to be turned into more detailed action plans with specific targets for the following year. The targets should specify the tasks involved and who will be responsible for them.
3. Provides space to plan the specific targets required to meet each priority.
4. Is devoted to detailed action plans for the year ahead.
5. Focuses on INSET and staff development needs arising from the plan.

A helpful checklist of issues are provided for schools to guide them in the preparation of priorities. The lists are not exhaustive but they interestingly reflect the aims and values of the authority, for example, in the emphasis given to the value of partnership with parents and the community. For example:

– Are policies documented and available for scrutiny by parents?
– Do teaching and learning styles reach out into the wider environment?
– Do National Curriculum schemes of work take account of equal opportunities?
– Schools must have regard to the domestic situation of their pupils.
– Schools must understand the diversity of domestic circumstances and should value and support them.
– The interactions between home and school, and between school and community must be examined.
– Schools must have known pastoral systems to help children and their families.
– Do parents know how to communicate with the school?

    – Should the school attempt to involve a wide cross-section of a school's community in the planning of its budget?

While it is acknowledged that 'marketing' will be an important part of any school's strategy in the new era, schools in Manchester are encouraged to focus more upon the advantages of 'communication' with parents and the community rather than upon competition. Schools are invited to consider the important following questions:

1. How is a parent (as a potential client) first introduced to the school? Is the school prospectus satisfactory, widely circulated and written in an appropriate, 'user-friendly' language?
2. How is important information about the school communicated to parents of new first years? What arrangements are there for parents of new first years to meet personally the members of staff most responsible for their child?
3. Are there sufficient opportunities for parents to talk to staff?
   - as a matter of routine;
   - at their own or the school's request.
4. What are the various kind of meetings held for parents? What proportion of parents come to each kind? Does the school have procedures for contacting non-attenders? Is every effort made to help parents feel comfortable when they come into the school?
5. Are complaints and difficulties consciously dealt with in a helpful way?
6. What sort of impression of the school are first-time visitors likely to receive? Are car parks clearly signed? Is the foyer attractive? Do all staff who come into contact with visitors appreciate the importance of creating a good impression? Do staff who answer the telephone do so in a way that will enhance the image of the school?
7. As visitors move around the school, are they likely to find the physical environment stimulating and attractive?
8. What is the relationship between the school and the community? Are pupils involved in any way with local community service? Does the school see itself as a focus for the community? How does/could it promote such an image?
9. Does the school have strong links with local organisation, industry and commerce? How could these links be improved?

10. What arrangements are there for publicising the achievements of the school and its students?
11. Has the school given special consideration to groups with whom to communicate; for example primary and post sixteen institutions, voluntary organisations, local parishes and faith communities etc.
12. Does the school have a press officer? Has the school a positive strategy to manage relationships with the media?

At the centre of the approach to make whole school development planning responsive to community and equal opportunity policies are strategies to reform the quality of teaching and learning, to which we now turn.

Teaching and learning in the 5–16 curriculum

Manchester believes that the National Curriculum provides opportunities for schools and the service generally to review and clarify educational priorities. The National Curriculum provides a minimum entitlement which should be developed and shaped by the emerging collective values of equality of opportunity and the participation of parents and the community. The implementation of the National Curriculum in Manchester will be developed to enable schools to respond to the needs of a particular set of pupils and their local experience. 'Only so will we be able to celebrate the rich ethnic and cultural diversity which the City has at its heart and in its history, and to build in the experience which local knowledge alone can offer. The LEA will continue to try to shape statutory provision to meet the particular needs of all its pupils.' The distinctive values of the Manchester service have shaped the aims of learning, curriculum development, and approaches to teaching and learning.

The aims of schooling

Since 1985 the LEA has based its curriculum upon 'agreed statements of collective purpose' in learning. (This forms a significant variation on the standard national model.) Schools should help pupils to:

- develop lively and enquiring minds capable of independent thought and the ability to question and argue rationally and to apply themselves to tasks;

- prepare for an adult world in which they participate as citizens;
- appreciate human achievement and aspiration and experience a sense of achievement;
- acquire respect for and understanding of other religions and moral values;
- understand the inter-dependence of individuals, groups and nations;
- experience responsibility and develop negotiating skills and exercise judgement;
- experience the school as a caring, supportive, learning environment, where there is equal opportunity regardless of sex, race, culture or disadvantage;
- foster enjoyment of learning that encourages them to take advantage of educational opportunities throughout life by the development of social, economic and political awareness.

An equal opportunity curriculum

The curriculum expresses the school's educational aims. It is the means by which they are carried into practice through the planning of learning experience. It involves the content and method of teaching as well as the expectations of teachers. It involves entering into a partnership with parents and the local community. The heart of the matter for each child is what she or he takes away from school and uses in his or her daily life that is the effective curriculum.

> Manchester's (whole) curriculum is based on the concept of equal opportunity for all pupils attending its schools. All pupils are entitled to a broad and balanced curriculum which introduces them to a range of coherent experiences of comparable opportunity and quality, irrespective of the type of school they attend, their level of attainment or social circumstances.
> Such a curriculum will be delivered within the positive policies which aim to ensure that entitlement is made into access so that pupils can actively contribute to their education and to wider society. There will be, for example, a continued need to combat stereotyping of all kinds and to engage pupils in social and moral issues by challenging structures which discriminate such as apartheid.

The LEA regards the National Curriculum as providing prescriptions of minimum entitlement that aim to ensure that all children have a broad and balanced education. The Manchester curriculum seeks to do more and ensure that children

- meet with experiences which make sense to them;
- have their difficulties understood;

- meet high and positive expectations of their promise as learners;
- find positive welcome for the richness of the multi-ethnic community of their schools and homes;
- are given the self-confidence to succeed.

Student centred teaching and learning

An integrated and balanced whole curriculum can only fulfil its aims of improving opportunity if delivered through approaches to teaching and learning which place the student at the heart of the learning process and expresses directly the values of equality. Teachers must:

- demonstrate the belief that all pupils can learn;
- emphasise positive achievement;
- make learning as practicable as possible to ensure the greatest access;
- manage the learning environment to enhance self-esteem, and celebrate achievement, by careful display and by encouraging cooperative approaches and shared activity.

The LEA encourages the adoption of a number of strategies to create a more accessible curriculum:

- examining the resources used in the classroom to eliminate sexist, or racist, language and images;
- increasing the cultural diversity of curriculum materials used with children and young people;
- including in the curriculum teaching about prejudice, bias, eg the changing pattern of women's working lives, discrimination in employment and the dual role parents may have to play;
- avoiding sexist/racist language and jokes and recognising the powerful effect language has in reinforcing damaging stereotypes;
- encouraging equal participation in all activities and being prepared to intervene to preclude domination by one sex or the other;
- expecting the same standards of work and behaviour from both girls and boys;
- ensuring that praise/blame is not gender associated;
- challenging assumptions that children have different abilities and aspirations because of their sex, racial origins or disability;
- monitoring what is actually happening in the classroom with a view to ensuring that children get similar amounts of the teacher's time and attention;

- providing positive role models for pupils through the types of responsibilities and activities undertaken by staff and by using other adults from the community to demonstrate the wide range of activities pursued by both women and men;
- examining the range of staff responsibilities to ensure that they are not gender-biased;
- initiating debate on all the issues which engages pupils, parents and teachers.

The service needs to ensure that all children learn in a supportive, stimulating and safe environment. Children should be encouraged to have high expectations of themselves and others, and to exploit to the full their learning opportunities. Each school must take seriously the concerns of its parents and their communities, and must seek ways of combating racism, sexism and the other forms of oppression.

Progression towards autonomy and responsibility

As students move through secondary education there is a growing emphasis upon preparing them for the 'adult world' beyond. The curriculum increasingly reflects the desire for young people to understand the relevance of what they are being taught and the need to test what they learn in environments other than those controlled by the school in work and in the community. The secondary curriculum reflects these transitions encouraging:

- teaching and learning styles which promote increasing autonomy and team responsibility;
- active learning experiences;
- assignments which increasingly have 'real world' consequences;
- increasing opportunities to meet and work with adults other than teachers;
- increasing opportunities for the exercise of responsibilities; including responsibilities for others within the community;
- opportunities to explore the world of work;
- contact with a greater variety of 'role models' in relation both to working life and adult life generally;
- access to advice and guidance, particularly in relation to careers;
- increasing opportunities to relate their school work to contexts out of school.

Manchester has taken a leading interest in a number of projects which seek to create a 'natural learning bridge' between school and post-16 learning opportunities:

- The Manchester Compact Ltd which seeks to forge close links between schools colleges and local employers;
- The technical and vocational education initiative, the national initiative that aims to make the curriculum more closely related to the world of work and adult life in general;
- Project Trident which focuses upon improving the quality of work experience.

These initiatives built upon the LEA's alternative curriculum strategies project designed to raise motivation and achievement amongst underachieving young people.

Recording and accrediting achievement

Particularly important for the aim of reinforcing achievement has been the authority's commitment to comprehensive forms of assessment which give credit to students for what they have accomplished. Manchester, like many other LEAs have developed records of achievement and pupil profiling which accredit achievement so as to reinforce motivation to learn, self esteem, and to encourage them to develop a broad range of personal qualities and skills. As with other aspects of the service in Manchester this system of assessment must be part of a whole school approach to learning and provide a coherent system for involving parents. To this end the Manchester Record of Achievement will provide:

- a basis for involving child, parent, and teacher as equal partners in the process of recording, reviewing and selecting achievements;
- a framework to enable teacher and parent to help the child to develop as an individual;
- a way of identifying with parental help the child's strengths and areas for improvement;
- a process by which parents can become aware of changes in the curriculum and classroom practice and can assist in the transfer of information between teachers and child.

Monitoring and evaluating performance

The authority believes that an essential part of effective school management is the capacity to monitor and evaluate performance. The intention is to maximise school growth and responsibility whilst demonstrating public accountability. The monitoring and evaluation of schools will reflect a partnership between school and the LEA in reporting on the curriculum, overall educational provision and local management. Schools will be expected to generate their own evaluative documents supported by the LEA, and the inspectorate team will undertake their own structured programme of visits to evaluate the progress which schools are making.

Information bases and performance indicators will be key to this process of 'auditing' schools. The LEA will require accurate and up-to-date information on the performance of schools in order to identify at an early stage if a school is in difficulties and in need of support and advice. 'The aim will be to avoid reaching a position in which the committee have a corrective role to play, perhaps to the point of withdrawing delegation'. A key management tool will be a set of indicators which enables governors and headteachers to monitor the impact of decisions about the deployment of resources and inform forward planning. These indicators are developed by schools with the advice and support of the LEA and seek to include both measures of efficiency as well as measures of effectiveness in terms of educational performance alongside other indicators which are less easily measurable, such as relationships between pupils and between pupils, staff and parents.

The indicators to be developed are to enable parents, governors and the education committee to monitor how effective schools are in delivering for pupils the highest standards of education within a rich and happy experience of school life. The performance indicators include an assessment of school performance in relation to the authority's own curriculum statement (Manchester 5–16) and other policy documents on, for example, sex education and school discipline. Each school's development plan will provide a statement of targets set and achieved. At the centre of Manchester's framework of evaluation are criteria that can be used to judge a school's effectiveness in achieving equal opportunities for all pupils. This entails, for example, the monitoring of learning outcomes as expressed through examination results.

The effectiveness of the implementing of the local management of schools scheme will also be monitored and evaluated. To this end the LEA, in consultation with governors and headteachers, is developing financial monitoring arangements, appropriate management information systems, and performance indicators for the financial and wider management functions of governing bodies with delegated budgets.

The whole scheme of evaluation will itself be thoroughly evaluated after its first three years of operation and recommendations prepared, if necessary, for its improvement. The LEA believes that a comprehensive approach to monitoring and evaluation of a school's progress requires the development of the 'whole school audit approach, when from time to time all aspects of a school's management, functioning and performance will be assessed by officers of the authority and after consultation with the school be reported to parents and the authority'.

Restructuring the education department

Expenditure has reinforced the emphasis within local management to reduce the size of the education department. In 1987, at the time of rate capping, the department was cut by about 19 per cent whereas the service level cut was about 8 per cent. In 1991–92 the department suffered a cut of 5.5 per cent which was a little below the level of cut for the service as a whole.

Cuts and the redistribution of functions have encouraged Manchester, like other LEAs to review the structure of their education department. Some change was inescapable: the department could not remain as it was. The 'shape' of the department would inexorably alter as strategic, evaluative and advisory tasks grew at the expense of clerical and administrative tasks. The review has considered key issues such as:

- the role and organisation of the inspectorate: while it was believed they had a major role to play in the new system it was not accepted that they should be a 'separate' branch of the department;
- the separation of client and contractor roles within the department, and the role of the department acting as a client on behalf of schools and colleges

The options included four models: a model of minimum disruption (four branches of schools, continuing education, resources, common services; each led by a Senior AEO); a model which divided the department into two divisions each led by a deputy education officer. One division, called Management (budgets, capital, personnel, information) and the other called Establishments (schools, CE, under fives, inspectorate); a model which divides the department into three divisions, schools and quality development, children's services; and continuing education and resources; lastly a model proposing radical restructuring into central (strategy, finance, information) and local (schools, under fives, inspectorate) services.

The LEA has chosen option 3 as an interim model for reorganisation on the assumption that planned organisation change would become a necessity through the 1990s. Any model chosen could not become a blueprint for the decade to come which requires adaptation to a new culture of permanent change.

PART 2 1991–92

Two issues in particular have dominated the LEA during 1990; one is the budget and the other is LMS in terms of actually working hard to get it right. A third issue has been an increasing focus upon quality control and a programme of audits will be beginning from October 1991. Two values have underpinned the response of the LEA to these issues; the first is importance of achieving value in the use of public money – 'you should spend public money as if it were your own, ie prudently, trying to get the best out of the money, staff and buildings. The second is an increasing orientation to publics service: 'we should not be doing things to people but with them and for them'.

Cutting expenditure

Cutting the budget has been a continual preoccupation for Manchester, consuming time and energy. In the last three years the education service has had to make £40 m of cuts. The 1990–91 budget was reduced by £15 m and in March 1991 preparing for the 1991–92 budget a further £5.3 m cut was required. Three months later in June, at short notice, officers were expected to take out of the budget another £3.5 m.

> The cuts have fallen on training initiatives, curriculum initiatives and the contingency fund (not for buildings, that comes out of a different fund, but for staffing, so that if there is an epidemic in the winter there will be little reserve money to pay for teaching cover). We have closed two colleges, we have closed the education development service. . . we have reduced the adult service by nearly 40 per cent we have reduced the youth service by something like 20 per cent; we have turned a lot of other services into income generators. We have reduced the museum service and the music service and there is charging introduced there as well. Now all of that has to be driven from here to make it actually happen, because budget saving on paper may seem quite easy, but to try and deliver them against a no redundancy policy means vast amounts of work; The whole thing in twelve months has been quite revolutionary.

The LEA's principal budgeting priority has been to protect school budgets. In 1990–91 school budget shares were not cut at all, while they have been cut 1 per cent for 1991–92. (Caretaking and cleaning had to be cut to prepare it for competitive tendering.)

So we have deliberately gone to protect school budget shares, not on the basis of any ideology of 7 per cent discretionary elements etc, but on the basis that those who need the direct services the most are the children and the deliverers of those services are the schools. Now, alright a lot of the other services are central to development, to good practice, to a lot of other things, but if you come down to those basics – what is the most important thing – it is getting a teacher in front of a class – it is as simple as that.

The LEA believes that it must now be approaching near the top of the LMS league in terms of: firstly, ' the amount that we delegate of the total, the psb – we delegate 86.2 per cent against a government target of 80 per cent and even their revised target for 1993 is 85 per cent' and secondly, 'also we are above government target in relation to distribution by pupil numbers'. Although this high delegation of resources to schools is partly an effect of the formula having to use the average rather than the actual costs of teachers, primarily it is a result of Manchester's chosen values of delegation. For this LEA is choosing to give schools more resources as part of their anti-poverty campaign 'a lot of the discretionary elements were to do with anti-poverty measures: it means that we are trying to make sure that we get more money into schools, to get the teachers in front of the classes: in a sense we have actually met government policy, but from an entirely different ideological reason.'

The LEA also prioritised protection for the pre-five service because 'that was probably one of the best ways which we could set about tackling the problems of poverty, and poverty related underachievement'. Protecting schools has meant cutting back on central administration and central services. Schools, it seems, are being trapped in a dilemma of wanting both to maximise their own resources yet at the same time wanting the benefit of the central services which they value and have become accustomed to using:

> One problem which I think is becoming more prevalent is that because we have cut some special services – like child guidance and other things – it means that the number of children, particularly in the high schools, who have severe emotional and behavioural problems, are now in mainstream schools when in the past they might be in some kind of service. At the same time, the social service department has been making cuts so they can't send these children off to residential establishments, they can't afford to, but keep them here. So that is one effect: to increase the problem of behavioural and emotional difficulties. . . The effect of the contraction of central services has cut the services to children in need.

The Chief Education Officer recalled a recent secondary heads meeting in which one head pleaded with him not to cut central services any further. The CEO pointed out with some irony that at the outset of the Education Reform Act it was in response to the heads wishes that school budgets were given priority.

> When I was challenged at a recent meeting of secondary heads, one of them said if you cut this and cut that we end up with problems, and I said hang on a minute, as I recall at the time when I laid out the principle, that we would not cut school budgets, shares will be protected you all agreed, you can't have it both ways. If you have a cash limited budget you have to choose; you choose; whether you have the money in schools, or you have the money in central services.
>
> Do you know for the first time in my life I have heard heads say don't cut Crown Square any more, don't cut the administration any more; we need your help, we need your support.

Towards tighter management of LMS

Manchester has taken to LMS. Although it would prefer a number of changes; to eliminate the market force and some of the employment practices, particularly in preventing the LEA from being the employer, 'but the basic principle of local management is to be commended: of local managers having the freedom to manage and having a budget which is free enough to allow them to do things within it'. Heads in a neighbouring LEA were complaining to a Manchester officer that they were being denied delegated responsibilities:

> I am not entirely convinced that all LEAs have come to terms with LMS. These heads gave a catalogue of examples of issues they were fighting for the LEA to delegate, which for me were not issues; bits and pieces to do with the budget or incentive allowances for example, I mean why should you from here want to specify the numbers, types and purposes of allowances which schools can deliver, when out there you have got people who know the strengths and weaknesses of their own staff and want to adjust for it, the needs of the kids etc, there is no point in trying to do that from here, it is pointless. It is not good management practice. Now from all I hear there are examples like that still around.

Getting the management of LMS right has been the LEA's second major priority, following the budget. Three issues have been important:

1. Accurate administration
The first issue has been to achieve precision and accuracy in terms of the detail of budget shares to ensure that the LEA fulfils its administrative functions effectively:

making sure that we get it right, and that we get it right in terms of the figures that we send out, that the budget shares are accurate, that the advice that we give is accurate, that we follow up in relation to bills on direct works, and do you know what I mean, that our accounts are accurate. Do you know what I mean all of the very bread and butter, administrative things, which if you don't get right you have no credibility; you can make every speech in the world but you must get these things right. This is something which education departments have just not concentrated upon in the past.

2. Organisational cohesion

The second important issue in achieving tighter management of LMS has been to achieve greater clarity in terms of the role and job responsibilities of officers within the department. People across the department were duplicating work in relation to schools, giving conflicting advice, while issues which needed response 'were falling between stools'.

Improving the accuracy of advice and the quality of service to schools required the education department to improve radically its own internal communication and cohesion of working: 'questions of who does what in relation to the services which we provide, sorting out within the department that people were duplicating, we were having issues fall between stools, that we were clear about the relationship between one part of the department and another . . . and unless you get common understanding you are going to get conflicting advice going out, therefore the need to communicate more effectively internally has never been more apparent because so many decisions were made separately here.'

The CEO was clear that this would be difficult to achieve given the history and culture of separate branch working in the department. In the past the advice schools received depended upon who they spoke to. The branches too often spoke from a different script. As the deputy put it: 'That has been a major task in turning the whole thing round, turning the whole department, all its officers, all its thinking round to working as one department rather than as separate Branches.'

Turning the department round has he says been 'quite revolutionary'. Officers in the department are now clear about what their responsibilities are within a branch, but they also know who else they can work with across the department. Cross departmental teams are formed which bring people together in different ways. The 'old branch divisions are collapsing all about us'. Morale and motivation, which are likely casualties in shrinking organisations have, purportedly, looked up.

the point now is, the way that management operates here, if you don't know the script, you know there is only one and you know there is a chance to have a rehearsal, you can go to rehearse it regularly so that you don't forget your lines. So there is a great deal of difference between what the past was and what to-day is and what we are trying to develop.

The senior management team have set the tone for a new style and culture of departmental working by meeting daily to review together the issues facing the department: each member of the team is encouraged to contribute to what may appear to be a specialist item:

> seven people, every day, nine o'clock we sit down most days its half past 8 and on the days when we are pushed its 8 o'clock. We sit down and we do issues affecting the whole department, so if I'm sitting there and its an FE issue that does not matter, or an adult issue, we are all tuned in to the whole department. Every day we also see all the letters that come in that are adressed to the CEO. We see the many agendas that people are raising, so that we are all tuned in to that and we all play a corporate part in that view of what is happening. That is every day. On Mondays we spend two hours together. And at a time like the budget time, like we are into now, we spend a lot of time together. That is how you start to get consistency.

Some enthusiasts were sceptical to begin with believing that it consumed time which could be better spent on the detailed specialist task in hand. But understanding of the indirect benefits of regular meetings gradually developed: 'it develops teamwork, consistency of approach'. Officers realised that if the Education Reform Act was to work it required a corporate approach from the department:

> the interesting thing for me was, where I had come from I was very task oriented, totally, I should have known better but what I had to learn was that if this thing was going to work in the context of the 1988 Act we would have to have a corporate view. I am now a far better manager as a result of sitting here with seven other people; now, looking at my particular task I realise that there are people who ought to be in with me on this who I can rely on to support me on a range of things; there is now much more working across these branches than I have ever known, Roy. And it actually happens, you don't have to clear lines, we just pop in and work with each other.

3. Further reorganisation

The cuts together with the growing understanding of the need for a corporate approach within the department to achieve its primary functions: strategic management and quality assurance. 'A further reorganisation was necessary where we have restructured yet again, so the time when we are trying to deliver all the statutory arrangements that we have to set in place we have had to be restructuring here. That has been pretty hard.'

4. Improving school management

The task of implementing the local management of schools has illustrated that schools, as much as the LEA, needed to improve their management. Schools have been seeking support from the LEA on a number of things: on staffing, discipline, curriculum, admissions and especially on management. Many heads have come through the ranks as excellent teachers and now find themselves as a head with little experience of, or training for, managing an organisation:

> A number of our heads have actually run away from the quality assurance approach in their schools: they have become bunkered, they have become office bound. They have developed a mental set which says that (LMS administration) is what the job is now thanks very much, my teachers will teach, and all the SATS will come and go, and I've got this thing called LMS and I've got these important meetings to go to. This is what we are sometimes seeing. Now the strong heads, the clear thinkers, those who have the right kind of view of what it is all about can cope with LMS on the basis that it is, well, a management issue, it is about making strategic choices, rather than becoming immersed in detailed administration all the time.

Officers were concerned that a number of schools were operating with weak management, 'where there is not the sharpness of delivery or internal self-evaluation etc, and it shows'. This anxiety has led to the third major issue dominating the work of the authority over the past twelve months or so: to improve the capacity for planning and quality assurance throughout the service.

Planning and monitoring for quality

The vehicle for improved planning and monitoring of performance at the level of the LEA is the education service plan, and at the level of the institution is the school (or college) development plan. The education service plan for 1991–92 was agreed by the committee in December 1990 and sets out the strategic and operational tasks which the department will address during the financial year. It sets out the objectives to be achieved, the action required, the target dates for realising those objectives, the outcomes the department is looking for, and it defines how the process is to be monitored and evaluated as a whole. These requirements for the service plan provided a framework for monitoring its progress. This will be monitored in June 1992.

One of the principal priorities in the plan is the implementation of the Manchester curriculum which sets out the entitlement of all children to all aspects of the curriculum. The National Curriculum is regarded as 'only a starting point' towards a whole curriculum which meets the needs of the child and reflects the aims and values which Manchester believes should inform education. The LEA is developing a philosophy of teaching and learning which emphasises cooperative learning in groups as well as cross curricular themes (such as health education, the performance arts, economic awareness). 'The National Curriculum may help in sharpening up the definition of a subject based curriculum and clarify targets but neglects reform of the learning process.'

It is the importance given to improving the processes of learning and teaching that is encouraging the LEA to emphasise profiling, which celebrates the achievement of young people, and the role of parents as partners in the learning process. Parents need to be involved and kept informed.

The revised *5–16 Curriculum For Manchester Schools* published in April 1991 will form the basis for a working party to be set up in the autumn of 1991 to agree 'success criteria' or performance indicators to monitor and evaluate the achievements of schools. Once the guidelines are agreed, schools will evaluate their own performance against the criteria and then the LEA will undertake an external evaluation. What is evaluated in any school will depend upon the objectives and targets set out in their three year development plan.

Manchester schools first produced development plans in 1986. Building on this experience during the winter of 1990, working groups of primary special and secondary headteachers in consultation with the inspectorate were set up to produce guidelines to help schools draw up their development plan for 1991–92 (stage 1) and for the following two years (stage 2). Within the plan schools are expected to identify their priorities and at stage 1 draw up action plans for each priority. The development plan would set the agenda for subsequent inspections with the LEA seeking to examine whether the school has been able to achieve the tasks which it had established as a priority for its own development.

Thus, while seeking to provide advice and support to heads in the management of schools the LEA is also learning to take a more detached 'critical friend' relationship with them. In the past officers believe that too many problems in schools were tackled by 'throwing money at it': issues of the quality of institutional management were rarely addressed. Now, the LEA is emphasising the importance of management and auditing the performance of schools: monitoring value for money as well as quality in the delivery of the curriculum. Such monitoring is followed up with open reporting to governors.

At the same time, it is clear that the LEA is devoting more time to working with heads as partners to develop the strategy, plans and criteria which are to shape the service as a whole. Key policy guidelines emerge from officer, adviser, head/teacher teams. Such partnership working had often been neglected in the past in what had been a top down culture of policy formation with the schools in a dependency relationship with Crown Square.

Post-16 education and training

Although a draft strategic plan had been prepared during the autumn of 1989 on post-16 education and training the level expenditure cuts required (£6.7 m) caused the report to be set aside in favour of a fundamental review of provision and priorities. The budget constraints meant the daft strategy could not be delivered. The review revealed a number of problems:

- over provision and staffing and the assumed continuation of four to five colleges;
- excessive resources (£1 m) being spent on management at the expense of course delivery;
- 20 per cent surplus capacity in terms of buildings;
- the need to separate youth, adult and FE services;
- an excessive amount of duplication and internal competition between the colleges.

What the budget exercise did was to expose a great deal of inter college squabbling, duplication and inter-college competition that was unnecessary. I don't mean that I want a system which is non-competitive but the real problem as far as the LEA is concerned comes from external forces such as other colleges, other LEAs and the private sector, such as Sight and Sound so the last thing we want is unnecessary internal competition.

The whole thinking behind that strategic plan, had to be revised. 'A cold hard look at our continuing education provision showed the need for a new strategy for post-16. . . The more we got into the budget exercise, the more we lifted the lid, the more I think we realised it was not working'. Very tough decisions had to be made and a new report on reorganising post-16 education and training was prepared.

What in effect the LEA did, and perhaps for the first time, was develop a strategic role in the sense of, one, determining how much money it was going to spend on FE, and secondly what it was going to spend its money on. For its money it wants to spend it on 'x' number of training courses in woodwork or whatever it is; and if you do that you then say to the college governors and management here is £20 m, here is what we want you to provide, how you do it, how you go about it, is now your responsibility and we will have criteria about how we will judge you. And what we previously said was here is £20 m fullstop.

The new strategy set out the curriculum/training areas to be provided; the resource levels and limits; the buildings and staff required; and how the plan was to be monitored and evaluated. The proposals included:

- reducing to two colleges;
- eliminating whole tiers of management;
- rationalising responsibility for a course programme on one site, with outreach in the other college if necessary;
- separating youth and adult from further education colleges.

The reorganisation plan was designed to prepare post-16 education and training in Manchester for the 1990s. But the Government's White Paper in 1991 undermines that ambition. The White Paper is said to be 'presumptuous and feeble'. It is presumptuous because it ignores many of the desired developments which have already been initiated by LEAs, and indeed assumes rather that LEAs have been preventing things from happening; and it is feeble because it is not radical enough in its proposals to break down the divisions between non-vocational and vocational qualifications. The agenda for change in Manchester includes:

1. to displace A level as the principal qualification for 16 to 19 year olds;
2. to achieve a more coherent interrelationship of the variety of qualifications – allowing progression and credit accumulation;
3. to enable greater variety of routes into higher education, 'rather than just the three A level type entry, because, I don't care what anyone says, it is still the 3 A level route which dominates'.

I would like to see a route which takes you through a wider variety of taking subjects, a combination of vocational and non-vocational, and there is nothing wrong in seeing models in which people can actually go off to work and come back into higher education and get their vocational or academic qualifications through a work experience route. There are a whole range of things you could do there which I don't think are being tackled. I don't think it tackles the questions of attracting more young people from working class areas, in particular areas where there are degrees of poverty, into further and higher education. There are not the financial incentives (such as educational maintenance allowances) and very often in inner city areas that is one of the things which is necessary.

So the White Paper, it is proposed, is defective in terms of educational philosophy. Its recommendations will also prevent effective educational planning and they will deny accountability and democracy:

> Colleges have not been as efficient or as effective as they should have been, but I don't believe the Government have come up with any proposals which actually make that much better. It is simply transferring from local to central control and if you ask me it will weaken it, because it throws out the whole element of planning. If you take local things like transition which is necessary and we have worked really hard at, I mean we have raised the staying on rates in spite of what the Government says. It is all right them standing up and saying they have raised the staying on rate; no they haven't, what have they done towards it. It is very much people on the ground, doing a lot of hard work in schools and colleges towards integrating each other, developing strategies like compact and other things which have actually got people to reconsider going on to further education. Those are things on the ground, not by people, making a speech. And that element will go; they will be seen as separate institutions, and the coordination by people at LEA level will not happen.. . I also think that the whole question of planning will go, you can't simply rely on market forces to do everything. It is a naive assumption. It is a naive assumption in relation to the modern economy, there has to be an element of planning. That means that either the planning has to be done by someone at the regional level and presumably a bureaucrat not accountable to anybody, or it does not happen at all. If it is a north west region how can they possibly know what the planning should be in relation to Moss Side and Hulme.

The growing loss of accountable planning of post-16 education and training is already exemplified in the operation of the training and enterprise councils. Although the TECs are believed to have potential their effectiveness depends upon them 'being freed from very centralised control. . . The shackles are still put on by the Department of Employment preventing the decentralisation of the system. The TEC boards are too constrained by former practices'. If the regeneration of the economic base, so important to a connurbation like Manchester, is to take place there must, it is argued, be a major public commitment to providing adequate training.

A note on opting out

No school has entered into any stage of the opting out process, not even a vote in the governing body of a school. A number of reasons are advanced for this interesting phenomenon: 'firstly, that

25 per cent of the schools are Roman Catholic and the Bishop of Manchester has issued a strong line that no Catholic schools will opt out. Indeed we have had only one sniff of opting out and it was an RC school: we heard that the school was visited and no more was heard of the process. Secondly, we have worked very hard at bonding the schools together, developing the idea of clusters of schools providing mutual support for each other and holding each other together – this might make it difficult for one school to break away. We have also devoted a lot of time to setting up networks of heads and of the office being visible in support of schools. Thirdly, the Labour Party has invested a lot of time informing its representatives on school governing bodies'. There has nevertheless, been occasional 'banter' from one or two heads about opting out as a means of applying some pressure upon the LEA, and officers would not be surprised, if the same Government is returned following the election, and there is the same constraint upon resources, then one or two schools might seek to opt out.

Conclusion

Manchester is willing to acknowledge that some of the legislative reforms are consistent with and can support their own agenda for the renewal of education. But they retain a firm conviction that if education is to be effective it must respond to the learning needs of particular groups of young people. The major task facing the City is the underachievement of disadvantaged children and the chosen strategy asserts that a commitment to equality, to involving parents and the community as legitimate partners in the service, together with the creation of student centred perspectives on teaching and learning can restore motivation and achievement.

Devolving responsibilities to governors and headteachers can help schools respond more effectively to the needs of their particular children and communities. But the quality of schools and the service generally depends upon each part of the service perceiving their interdependence working towards shared values of equality and quality in learning. Working together as partners, each can enhance their own progress as well as that of the whole service.

The distinctive achievement in Manchester has been to develop understanding within the department as much as across the service generally that cost-conscious and efficient management is not only consistent with but a condition for radical educational objectives. Public resources prudently planned, deployed and evaluated for their effectiveness is the best means of achieving public purposes in education. The leadership of the chief education officer in introducing a sharper system of management seeks to ensure that all work as a cohesive team providing consistent, accurate advice and coordinated support for schools and colleges.

Yet the expenditure reductions are likely to undermine the benefits of what has been achieved. While the cuts have undoubtedly squeezed out wasteful use of resources and staff they are also damaging services, including central support services, which are indispensable to the quality of the City's schools. The conditions for supporting the new efficient management of education in Manchester are being denied the resources needed to enable the new system to flourish.

6
Warwickshire County Council
For strategic management of quality and accountability

PART 1 THE NEW CONTEXT OF CHANGE AND OPPORTUNITY

Warwickshire believe that the changes required by the Education Reform Act provide an opportunity to enhance the quality and accountability of the service. There are potential tensions in the changed set of relationships, powers and responsibilities between central government, the authority, diocesan authorities, schools, colleges and other providers. The reforms imply two models of quality and accountability that sit uneasily together: one emphasising 'connoisseurship' and judgement (as in the National Curriculum) and the other, taken from the commercial world, is the 'private contractor model' which emphasises the power of the customer. Yet the formidable challenge and great sense of opportunity is to keep these two models in balance without rejecting either out of hand.

> The Education Reform Act has presented us with the opportunity either to give up the ghost and allow the centralising and market place tendencies of the Act take over, or to grab hold of the Act and make it work in and for Warwickshire. We have chosen the latter course of action, and do so in the belief that there is a good chance that both the quality of education and the culture of accountability will flourish.

Central to the Warwickshire perspective is the belief that learning quality and accountability are properly at the forefront of educational policy and that excellent management is the key to achieving those ends. 'Our central belief is that provision of high quality education represents the essential purpose of accountability. We believe that this starts and ends with the pupil or student and his or her teacher or lecturer . . . as in all accountabilities a two way process operates . . . Throughout this network of accountabilities, the provision of high quality education is the glue that secures coherence, shared values and success.'

To express an interpretation of the reforms in this way begins to point up the necessary interconnections between a number of purposes and the means of achieving them. The key to any successful implementation of the reforms is to perceive the way they hang together as a system. One of the distinctive qualities of the Warwickshire approach is the intellectual frame of reference which is brought to bear upon the task of managing change. The County Education Officer, an advocate of the Grubb Institute's commitment to the benefits which system's theory brings to the quality of practice in management, has developed a 'mental systems model' to interpret the process of managing change. Systems thinking encourages analysis of the component parts of the system, the tasks and authority that define their relationships to each other and the whole, and the nature of the boundary between the system and its environment. It is essential to any understanding of a system to perceive it as a process of transformation the excellence of which depends upon its capacity to evaluate the quality of the output in a way that 'feeds back' into an understanding of the 'inputs' required.

Such a framework makes good sense of the management task facing LEAs striving to implement the education reforms. The task of the service is to transform the quality of learning of its clients, and to formulate a comprehensive and useful means of reporting to the public on the performance of the system. The capacity of the system to learn from the public feedback on these accounts will characterise the extent of its effectiveness, while the condition for becoming effective will depend upon clarifying the internal roles and working relations within the system. Warwickshire has developed a very clear understanding of the distinctive roles and tasks within the new management of education. It is to these that the discussion now turns.

Understanding new roles, powers and responsibilities

The distinctiveness of the Warwickshire approach is the clear vision they have developed about the roles and responsibilities of the new

LEA. Far from believing the LEA is weakened or undermined by the legislation, they propose that the LEA has the key role of strategic leadership in enabling the new system to realise its purposes of learning quality and accountability. The LEA will take a leading role in clarifying the educational values that will inform policy making, resource targeting and development planning.

> We want a value based policy framework, though it must lead us into manageable targets.
> The LEA should have, and Warwickshire does have, a view about the purpose of education in its schools and colleges. The idea is that the LEA's policy statement shapes and influences the allocation of resources of different kinds, the preparation of school and college development plans and the process, form and content of monitoring. Likewise, each of these, with and through a feedback mechanism, cumulatively influence the policy statement.

In short, it is this process of strategic management that creates the leadership role for the LEA. In the past many in Warwickshire believed 'policy a nuisance, impossible in such a diverse county.' Now, 'the policy statement is the linchpin of our proposed model' because of the opportunity which it provides to lead and coordinate the system. Given this understanding of its role, the management challenge facing the LEA in a rapidly changing context is to develop:

- the new system of functions between the LEA, governors and institutions;
- shared values about the purposes and quality of learning;
- more strategic policy planning, goal setting, monitoring and reporting;
- quality in teaching and learning within schools, colleges and centres;
- performance monitoring, evaluation and accountability;
- organisational development within the department as well as within the system as a whole including collaborative working between officers and advisers to provide efficient and effective services to schools and colleges.

The particular functions of the LEA in the new system are to:

- establish, with governors and staff of schools, colleges and other education providers, a policy framework within which all may be enabled to effectively operate delegate powers;
- support and advise schools and colleges so that they can achieve agreed objectives and targets as well as ensuring that they are fully aware of both legislative requirements and good practice nationally and in Warwickshire;

- plan across the system as a whole so that there are sufficient resources and facilities available;
- allocate resources, mainly according to agreed formulae but also including capital building programmes and small grants in line with agreed policy objectives;
- ensure that teachers and LEA staff are provided with appropriate opportunities for professional development, including an agreed staff appraisal process;
- monitor, evaluate and inspect the quality of work in an open and shared way with schools and colleges;
- provide comprehensive information concerning the opportunities available and the performance of Warwickshire's educational system.

These functions are seen to represent the major responsibilities of the authority in the changing circumstances of the 1990s.

While the authority clarifies understanding of its new role, governors of schools and colleges will increasingly assume responsibilities and powers which have traditionally rested with the authority. These include the appointment of staff, deciding the number of staff required for different purposes, the programme of internal decoration and maintenance, and the virement of budget between staff, maintenance, equipment, books etc. The development of self-managing institutions is the major objective of the local management of schools and local management of colleges schemes. Similar developments are being introduced for community education because the authority is firmly committed to the principle of decision-making 'nearest the client'.

The new relationship between the LEA and its self-managing institutions is illustrated in the transactions between them over resources:

These transactions will often, in future, be based on the concept of the authority as client and the school or college as contractor. For example we will have an LEA policy initiative, linked to a budget for the promotion of community education, and have another relating to pupils and students with special educational needs. We will want to ensure that the resources available for these policies go to the contracting establishments . . . which are most likely to fulfil the policy objectives concerned. However, of course, many services such as libraries, supplies, repair and maintenance, will operate increasingly on a trading basis where the authority is the contractor and the school or college is the client. The value and quality of these services will be decided by the schools and colleges operating in their client or customer role.

What holds the new system together in spite of the differentiation of roles and functions is the commitment to establish a framework of shared values, purpose and policy objectives.

The framework of values and purposes

Warwickshire believe that the development of the service should be shaped by a shared understanding of educational purpose and of the values that will inform the making of policy and the setting of policy objectives. 'Values and a statement of policy form the linchpin of our proposed model and, in Warwickshire, we preceded all of our ERA consultations with this premiss.' The overriding value and purpose of the service has been defined as:

> The fundamental purpose of the education service is to ensure that sufficient high quality education is provided, appropriate to the interests, needs and entitlements of the people of Warwickshire, enabling pupils and students to contribute with confidence to their own future development, their family, workplace and community.
>
> In our scene setting aims statement we refer to the primacy of educational quality and to the nature of the new partnership. Implicit in this notion of partnership is a range of accountabilities of a mutual kind.

The particular values and policy objectives which have been chosen to shape the education service as it moves into the 1990s are:

- the most important client is the pupil or student, as well as the parent; 'we decided that if the term client was to be used, and that was a contentious issue, then for us the main client is the pupil or student';
- education is centrally concerned with the development of the whole person, which means that education has to meet personal, social and vocational needs as education is for life;
- the particular educational needs of pupils and students who are socially or economically disadvantaged or who have learning difficulties or disabilities should be positively recognised;
- a well trained and committed staff is the key resource in providing a high quality service;
- the accountability of providers to both clients and the local electorate is best achieved by combining quality with the most effective use of resources;
- the education service must be flexible and responsive to the changing needs and rising expectations of its clients;
- the education service flourishes when it is based on partnership and mutual respect between clients, elected members, officers, diocesan representatives, staff and governors.

These values and objectives are then used to inform the process of strategic policy planning.

Strategic planning

'There is a need for a planning system which makes sense of the myriad parts of the whole. Demographic forecasts and plans for new or extended buildings need to be combined with financial and business plans, identifying opportunities for cooperation and maximisation of resources across areas of the county or between groups of schools and colleges are also part of the authority's strategic role. Whilst more detailed management takes place in schools, colleges and elsewhere, the authority seeks to ensure that for all 16–19 year olds, for example, there is sufficient high quality provision available (whether in sixth forms or in colleges), or that in adult, youth and community education, no particular group is neglected or unfairly treated and that the scarce resources available are effectively used. Longer term strategies with policy implications are also prepared by the authority for widespread consultation and then for consideration and resolution by the full county council. Current examples of these include the development of an under fives strategy, the optimum age of transfer between primary and secondary school and the change from a three to four term academic year.

In these ways, quite significant and weighty issues are taken on board and are subject to local democratic scrutiny. The issues are frequently those which require coordinating over time and space with hundreds of small organisations covering over 765 square miles. The authority's strategic role is a good example of the undoubted need to invent a local authority if one didn't already exist!'

Policy priorities

In the 1990s the education department will need to:

- work with schools and colleges to agree targets and to monitor their effectiveness in meeting them;
- seek to obtain the resources to provide the education service that we and the public see as necessary and desirable;
- ensure that irrespective of gender, ethnicity, age or disability, the education is equitably and widely accessible;
- offer all people a wide range of educational opportunities applicable to their identified needs;

E

- ensure that staff have wide-ranging support and in-service training;
- provide to schools and colleges expertise and advice which responds to their needs, eg on matters of curriculum, finance, staffing and public relations;
- establish a network so that good practice, sound ideas and news on all educational developments can be identified, disseminated and exchanged;
- accept ultimate responsibility for the quality of education in Warwickshire.

Such priorities are developed into targeted policy plans for each year; for example, to improve the quality of primary education by redirecting £2 m from elsewhere in the education budget, to ensure the development of coherent 16–19 provision, to ensure the elimination of surplus school places, and so on. In this way, policy defines the management of resources.

Resource management

In Warwickshire the allocation of resources and the development of LMS are firmly linked both to the authority's policy statement and to the development plans of school and colleges. 'Formula funding is one, albeit important, part of the resources we have available. Pump priming LEA grants for LEA initiatives, combined with central government grants (such as ESGs and LEATGs) should also be part of the policy driven allocation of resources. Support and advisory services represent a further and very important resource which need to be targeted in line with stated policies.'

> Resources have to be allocated not merely on the basis of how many pupils or students there are available, but in relation to educational and curricular needs. We also reminded ourselves that there are the continuing needs of youth and adult education, provision for the under-fives, arts, museums, the careers service and so on, and that these must not be ignored. Particular resource allocations should be linked to the development of community education, special needs, the primary phase and, of course, provision for 16–19 year olds. So we are beginning to raise here key priorities in terms of our objectives . . . Finally . . . it is important to confirm that the services provided by the authority to schools and colleges, as our clients, will be firmly based on value for money.

Teachers and lecturers are the key resource. At the centre of the educational business for Warwickshire is the teacher and this understanding creates one of their most important objectives:

> To recognise that for students, pupils and parents, it is the effectiveness of teachers and lecturers that is the key to the achievement of high standards. The essential role of managers, administrators and advisors, is to support, encourage and enable teachers and lecturers to perform as effectively as possible.

The significance of this objective is to ensure that the teaching resource is effectively developed, provided with systematic training, which is based upon a proper identification of assessed needs.

The local management of schools and colleges

Warwickshire welcomed the principle of local school-based management and believed that it would strengthen the partnership between the individual school and the authority. School budgets would be determined by formulae based on need rather than on historical patterns of expenditure and within the curriculum plan agreed with the LEA schools will have greater opportunity to plan the use of resources in response to the needs of pupils, parents, the local community and employers. 'LMS is an opportunity to review the policy as well as the financing of the service.'

The response of the authority to LMS was planned by a project team led by a seconded secondary headteacher and including advisers and officers with expertise in finance, law and information systems. This team reported to a steering group which represented all parts of the service affected by the changes. The orientation to the preparation of the scheme was to be schools oriented and not over determined by financial issues. A pilot project with eight schools provided invaluable experience about historic patterns of expenditure.

The authority planned to ensure that all schools would by April 1990 be funded on the basis of the county's formula regardless of whether they had received the delegated powers over staffing and financial management. Schools would be phased in to the LMS scheme: all secondaries by 1991 and all primaries (irrespective of size) by 1993.

The LEA took the view that it should delegate every allowable item of expenditure to schools either immediately or within a reasonable timescale. A number of items would be excepted from delegation initially (for example, major repairs, statemented pupils and specific units, educational psychology and welfare services, peripatetic music teachers, advisory teachers, the school library and museum services. LEA initiatives and community education, etc) but these would be kept under review. 'There was a sea-change of attitudes over time so that people got more enthusiastic about delegation, shouldn't we even get below 7 per cent, they began to say.' There was agreement amongst heads about not delegating the psychological and welfare services but disagreement about the music service. 'At least LMS makes clear the pattern of resourcing and allows public debate about it . . . LMS has made all parts of the service evaluate every aspect of the service.'

The formula was a significant influence in this process. It was perceived as a welcome, though painful, opportunity to re-examine and justify resource patterns amongst pupil age groups and types of school in order to arrive at a distribution that responded to the educational needs of pupils at their different ages. The formula would have to be much more sensitive than historic patterns of expenditure to the fundamental importance of the primary phase of education, while it was increasingly difficult to justify educationally small sixth forms when these students required a full range of learning opportunities. The formula linked to other LEA strategies would have to ensure that the needs of the 16 to 19 age group were addressed as a whole. Options were calculated for variations in age-weighted pupil units: the chosen option produced a movement to primary schools. The project team believed that research was needed to discover in more detail the learning needs of the different age phases and what it really costs to educate, for example, a five year old.

Perhaps the main issue of debate in the project team focused upon the factors which should determine the distribution of that proportion of the aggregated schools budget (ASB) not accounted for on the basis of age weighted pupil numbers (78.6 per cent). The factors chosen related to premises (6 per cent), split sites (1 per cent), small school size (9 per cent) and socio-economic (5 per cent) factors. The socio-economic factor was calculated on the basis of relative difference among schools based on the provision of free school meals. Some officers were unhappy with this indicator believing it far too crude a measure of deprivation.

The project team were particularly impressed by the spirit of collaboration which the process of consulting upon and implementing LMS was generating, 'the spirit is good, people supporting each other, sharing professional insights. Our strategy is to encourage collaborative activity, for schools to share staff, bursars, the delivery of the curriculum, INSET, and clerks to governing bodies. They need to share resources. This community spirit can overcome the pressure of market forces. It is beginning'. Cooperative working would, it was hoped be encouraged by the process of development planning in which the LEA invested much significance for strategic planning of the system as a whole.

School development plans

Development planning for schools as well as the LEA is regarded as indispensable to the management of change following the ERA, 'the linchpin in terms of the maelstrom of changes and initiatives'. The process of development planning can serve to hold together and integrate the disparate aspects of change. Policy priorities are identified, resources targeted, and progress towards implementation monitored and evaluated against performance criteria.

Schools are expected to work within an annual planning cycle informed by its policy statements and linked to a continuous process of review. This annual cycle will reflect the school's priorities which reflect the influence of both LEA and central government policies.

Within this process the most important consideration should be given to the school's own specific needs and demands and the authority has been developing a continuous needs assessment process to shape development planning. The assessment includes the school's own self-review mechanisms as well as the LEA's monitoring and evaluation system.

> Resource allocation will then follow, not preceed (!), policy in school development plans. And whilst the formula will determine the bulk of the resources, the linking of key policies to additional resources will be important and these resources will include people as well as money. So in addition to the key LMS formula we might also envisage bidding arrangements for additional resources or negotiating a mechanism which will include the allocation of central government grants and also LEA grants and support. Pump priming will be marginal in financial terms, but . . . increasingly significant in terms of policy.

A secondary school, for example, might have set itself the objective of improving post-16 participation rates over a three year period with targets negotiated with the LEA. The authority might then allocate cash as well as officer time (perhaps an adviser or careers officer) in support of the school's objective. Thus 'our policy statement and our 16–19 development fund are harnessed to an assessment of the school's objectives and their needs (in a manner) which is likely to promote educational quality and accountability'. Such school development planning within Warwickshire has built upon a longer tradition within further education.

Strategic planning of further education colleges

Warwickshire had anticipated the introduction of local management of colleges: 'we were already moving in that direction, and there was a willingness to embrace the underlying philosophy of dele- gated management'. The authority had been developing a process of strategic planning leading to formal contractual relationships with the colleges. With delegated management the role of the LEA focuses upon strategy, support of the colleges and advice on management expertise.

Much time was invested in preparing a strategic planning cycle for further education based upon consultation with the colleges. The approach has been distinguished by a commitment to continue the authority's tradition of basing staffing and resourcing in curriculum planning although the emphasis on numbers in the LMC formula makes this difficult. Building upon, but adapting the planning guidelines used in work related development planning, the LEA has prepared a plan in three parts: a strategic plan, an action plan and a performance document.

(i) The strategic plan

The strategic plan was formulated in consultation with the colleges, although the tight timetable constrained the extent of involvement. The plan articulated values of providing service and support to the community and groups that were disadvantaged traditionally and did not participate in the system; to the world of business; and to meet the needs of individuals, who have a right to express their goals and have them taken into account. Such objectives imply different kinds of provision and the need for greater flexibility in the system to enable access. 'It means removing the barriers and offering better guidance and support'.

Responding to the needs of diverse clients at the same time can lead to contradictions: serving more effectively both the needs of employers and individuals can potentially lead to difficult choices, furthermore, can the college serve every kind of need and remain economically viable – should they 'stick to their knitting'; yet to encourage colleges to stick to a particular kind of provision can point up tensions between the powers of the LEA and colleges. Joint working and planning has contributed to such tensions being discussed and, usually, resolved.

(ii) Action planning

Action plans were negotiated jointly with colleges and informed by the college development plan. The LEA expected that the action plans would follow a proforma and set out objectives (which expressed how the colleges would take forward the authority's mission), targets for achieving them on a annual basis, the programme of staff development, and criteria for monitoring and evaluating achievement. The plan was negotiated by a local inspector and officer and once agreed it was run through the computer to determine the resource implications.

Although there were inevitably tensions between the LEA and colleges in formulating plans there was also mutual interest in sharing information: 'we have said to the colleges that we don't wish to determine self-financing colleges, but we do need to know what you are doing. The colleges have indicated that they are pleased to be asked. They want the LEA to know that they may have to subsidise a course which is being sponsored by the Training Agency (as it then was): they want the prospect of the LEA's support in negotiating with such bodies as well as the authority's own funding in support of, for example, students with special needs . . . But to make judgements about funding particular courses the LEA has to know the totality of a colleges budget so that the distribution of resources is balanced and equitable'.

> So far there is not much opposition to the LEA saying it can set policy on say equal opportunities or special needs, on strategic issues that is. But it is when you get down to quantitative statements about what will happen where difficulties will arise, because a lot of our levers have been taken away. The DES has even prevented us talking about the colleges as *our* colleges.

It is recognised that it may take time to develop agreed conventions about managing the market collaboratively. The LEA has now no powers over detailed course approval and although funding may provide some leverage it will not provide control. The task for the LEA is to discover the 'fine line of influence' over the new system while the challenge for the college is, when the market develops, to 'learn to come together and say we need to negotiate': 'recent meetings of governors showed some indications that colleges are willing to collaborate'.

If the influence of the LEA in further education cannot depend upon finance it would have to depend upon good information systems:

> The role of the LEA ought to be managing the market, what is it if it is not that! But that will be difficult given the role of the TECs. The LEA now does not have many mechanisms of influence on the level and distribution of provision. That is why management information is so crucial, for market intelligence. Without this it is difficult to see whether the LEA can play any driving role in provision.

The role of the LEA may become 'a residual role on behalf of the clients'. Yet the DES have insisted that home to college transport is a delegated item: 'why is this not like awards for us to allocate to the students – it is things like this which undermine the strategic role of the LEA'. Frustrations such as these are perhaps the inevitable experience of negotiating respective roles and tasks in the new management of further education.

(iii) Performance document
A monitoring and evaluation document which explains and analyses the outcomes achieved. This has involved clarifying performance indicators for the service (and the difficult task of agreeing criteria which are acceptable to the Department of Employment as well as the DES. The development of indicators has been informed by the LEA's overall determination to create a framework for analysing the performance of services.

Learning quality: implementing the National Curriculum

Senior officers and inspectors are approaching the National Curriculum positively. They believe it often provides a useful framework for planning and one which requires to be elaborated and developed locally if it is to work effectively: 'we are not merely implementing the National Curriculum, we are about mediating and interpreting it to meet the needs of young people in Warwickshire'. Quality in teaching and learning will only be achieved by responding to the way children learn and using the National Curriculum more as representing a set of guidelines, rather than as a straight-jacket, to check whether programmes of study have been completed.

> We have not found significant difficulties in working with the NC – for example in English, if you unpack it, all you want to do is there. It does not preclude the practices we want to advocate. Although we are not sure about the technology or history reports, we find maths, science and English all helpful.

The distinctive interpretation of good teaching and learning which is being used to mediate the National Curriculum is not regarded as being unique to Warwickshire. Rather, it is a view which has developed from HMI papers and seminars and is promoted as good practice by professionals in a number of LEAs.

> The Warwickshire view of quality focuses on programmes of study rather than attainment targets. (We are concerned that teachers may focus on

what is to be tested and work back to what is to be studied.) We are child centred. We see education as a process of 'drawing out' as well as 'putting in'. We do think children learn best when

- doing not merely memorising;
- learning through first hand experience;
- encouraged to use their imagination;
- encouraged to experiment with a variety of responses;
- allowed time to produce work of quality and depth;
- engaged 'actively' in their learning;
- they exercise choice in learning;
- they take responsibility for their learning.

Such a process places the emphasis upon children learning rather than teachers teaching. These values lead us to look at the worrying things in past practice: an over reliance on published schemes of work; too much front of class teaching; too much closed learning – that is children being asked questions that imply 'right' or 'wrong' answers with too little exploration, speculation and diversity of inquiry. There has, moreover, been too little opportunity for group work and discussion, and too much emphasis on pupils working alone. Good practice involves group work to plan, challenge, support, help and amplify the learning process. This does not mean that group work is a panacea – a 'best thing since sliced bread'. But it frequently is undervalued as a learning strategy. We find that good teachers use a range of methods as appropriate: individual, pair, group and whole class, according to the nature of the activity. Excessive reliance on any of these denies learning opportunities to children.

Towards quality in teaching and learning

There is both a belief that a distinctive philosophy of what constitutes good education is emerging in Warwickshire as amongst the profession nationally, and also that shared agreement amongst the partners about the purposes and processes of learning is essential to quality in teaching and learning.

- Education is centrally concerned with the development of the whole child.
- All children are of equal worth and deserve equal opportunities.
- However, children are different and their needs show considerable divergence.
- Thus, effective classroom practice starts with the needs of individual children.
- Continuity and progression should be ensured for each child.
- High expectations of children.
- Close consultations with parents is essential, based on a recognition of them as prime educators in their own right.

The key to learning quality is seen to lie in a number of key processes that inform the practice of good schools:

- active learning;
- experience-based learning;
- imaginative thinking;
- guidance and counselling;
- a negotiated curriculum and contract learning;
- profiles and records of achievement that provide positive feedback;
- multi-agency curriculum;
- development and delivery.

Warwickshire have, therefore, been creating a clear understanding of what is valued in teaching and learning and formulating appropriate policies for governors, teachers and parents. The management challenge for the LEA has been to accommodate the national reforms to curriculum and assessment while retaining a distinctive vision about the process of education in Warwickshire.

The management of curriculum change

Initially, it was felt that teachers, especially in primary schools, were unhappy at the prospect of the National Curriculum: 'there was resentment against an imposed curriculum when the experience of teachers was of parents expressing appreciation and admiration. More subtly teachers resented the eroding of what was seen as a traditional part of their professionalism: that is, making decisions about the nature and process of learning. This was now being taken out of their discretion and there was a belief that this was to treat them as operatives, just implementing a given curriculum. So initially, the National Curriculum was not popular. But the working party reports, especially the TGAT report, and now the statutory orders reassured teachers and commanded a measure of support in schools, while the National Curriculum Council had been seen to stand up against political pressure to impose a narrow grammar school curriculum'. Advisers came to recognise that although the description of the curriculum was often not helpful, and they would have preferred HMI's focus upon 'areas of experience', nevertheless they came to understand that there was much overlap between the National Curriculum and county policy.

> we developed the view that the National Curriculum can be integrated with good practice in the county and enhance it; because we, schools, have been culpable of not carefully enough planning, monitoring and recording what is being learned. This can be enhanced by having a clearer framework.

Anxiety remained, however, about how the National Curriculum was to be implemented. 'It has been unsatisfactory. The whole thing was set in train in a way we would not have wanted, firstly because it was set out in subjects and secondly because of the scale and pace of change required.' The LEA has played an essential role in mediating and interpreting what was being expected of schools. They believed that there was no intrinsic difficulty in working with the National Curriculum, though advisers preferred a focus upon programmes of study rather than attainment targets ('our view is that learning quality lies in the programmes of learning whereas we are worried that teachers may have to identify what is to be tested and work back to the process of teaching').

Yet the survival strategies adopted by the advisers contained within them important principles for approaching the implementation of the national curriculum. 'A lot of our strategy has been to reassure teachers that they can't have it all up and running on day one. They have to look at what is common across the subject documents, for example the importance of encouraging children to ask questions rather than expecting them to inculcate facts, starting from what the children do and know in everyday experience and work outwards from that. Teachers should start with the common processes of learning rather than doing 'English' or 'maths' or 'science' in discrete boxes which start at fixed times in the day. It is difficult to get teachers to see, for example, that science is also a language activity because of the importance of accurate description, while a visit to an historic building can involve a number of related learning activities: understanding the past, mapping, measurement, talking and writing. Teachers should then go to the documents to check which learning activities have been completed, which omitted. We are encouraging teachers to think of the curriculum as activities and experiences rather than subjects, to be flexible in how they arrange the process of learning so that they have clear objectives for a lesson but are able to respond to children's enquiry':

> So we are using the National Curriculum documents as an analytical retrospective check list. We are saying to teachers, start with activities in a holistic way and then go to the documents to check what has been accomplished . . . We want teachers to identify what is good and what they are proud of in their practice and to build on what they have been doing. They need to hold onto this, a foundation on which they can build – they must not scrap all that they have been doing and go back to the beginning. That would be fatal.

This perspective indicated that even if a National Curriculum was to be implemented effectively it required the classroom teacher, the school and the LEA to develop a clear view about what they were trying to achieve in the process of teaching and learning. The curriculum had to be developed bottom up even to accommodate a national framework. Advisers hoped that this would be realised through the process of school development planning which should be curriculum centred and grow out of a realistic assessment of where a school is at and what it can achieve.

The authority's advisers worked from the outset to support the manifest need which teachers and schools were expressing for clear guidelines for implementing the National Curriculum. Any such guidelines presupposed of a shared county wide view of quality in learning. A tradition of inspectors working in quite an isolated way made this a new and difficult management task. Implementing the National Curriculum forced colleagues to come together and work out a common approach to implementation: a National Curriculum planning group and a curriculum and assessment team were formed. Anxieties were being expressed at the outset about how the separate subjects could all be implemented: but discussion enabled advisers to think through their approach:

> at one meeting the geographer was talking about basic skills within the subject and the science adviser said that they were also science skills. It was a seminal moment. It was perceived as a moment when the discussion moved beyond the subject to skills, attitudes and processes. We discovered a lot of agreement.

This encouraged advisers to re-examine the LEA's *Policy Statement on the Curriculum* and prepare a document for consultation which clarified the principles that informed the distinctive county approach to learning quality: The document *On Quality* describes the characteristics of a good school, its curriculum, classroom practice and mode of assessment. This was the subject of widespread discussion and negotiation. While differences of emphasis remained, a shared LEA view began to emerge and shape important policy documents, such as *Planning for Children's Learning in the Primary School*, inform in-service training, and be communicated in county wide bulletins, as well as talks to governors and parents. Indeed the county's documents on the National Curriculum and assessment have been regarded as exemplary regionally: 'they have been very well received: heads find them useful, teachers read them and our HMI tells us he recommends them all over the West Midlands as best practice in the National Curriculum'.

While teachers began to come to terms with National Curriculum, the companion assessment procedures presented more deep seated concerns for them. 'What they are really unhappy about is assessment. Although they have always assessed, the use of targets is new. Teachers are horrified at the scale of the demands involved

in teacher assessment because it is simply impossible – there is not
the time, nor the skills – where does one look to find the expertise
in this. There are 32 attainment targets in one particular subject,
four statements of attainment at each level for each key stage . . . In
maths there will be 60 assessments per teacher for every class of
pupils a week . . . and then there are the external requirements
of standard attainment targets which the teachers fear will take
precedence and in time lead to crude pencil and paper tests.'

> Such assessment linked to open enrolment and formula funding will
> create competitive pressure on schools. A crude market place mechanism
> will be substituted for a sophisticated process of making judgements
> about the quality of schools.

This background to the reforms placed pressure upon the LEA to
create indicators of performance which enabled the sophisticated
learning objectives of schools to be assessed in their appropriate
context without being reduced to crude quantitative statistics.

Performance and accountability

At the centre of Warwickshire's framework is a commitment to
improving the quality and accountability of the education service
and its institutions. The priority is to identify and understand
effective schools and the conditions which cause them to be so.
The LEA has established a number of policy objectives to facilitate
'an audit' of how the system is performing:

- to establish a monitoring system through which the educational, financial and personnel-related performance of schools
  colleges and other providers of services (including the authority's own administration) can be comprehensively described
  and based upon an understanding of the authority's central
  aim of ensuring that the highest standards of provision are
  delivered;
- to establish effective 'early-warning' systems in order that the
  monitoring system does not identify problems too late for
  effective remedial action to be implemented;
- to establish an effective and understandable liaison system
  between institutions (heads, principals and governing bodies)
  and the authority (education committee, administration and
  the inspectorate) so that the monitoring system is seen to be
  coordinated and open to continuous review and amendment;
- to establish a public system of reporting upon the performance
  and characteristics of the education service as a whole and

of schools and colleges in particular; to investigate the most effective means whereby such a system is made understandable and useful to clients;

- to establish a complaints procedure for parents and for students over the age of sixteen, based on simplicity, fairness and openness, and which encourages informal contact in the first instance;
- to ensure that the monitoring, reporting and complaints procedures fully involve all participants, whether providers or clients, lay or professional.

Such a system is designed to underpin the commitment to learning quality. The system also emphasises 'the relationship of mutual accountability between the authority and schools and colleges . . . We look to reporting as a feedback mechanism, a means of informing our wider public in Warwickshire, a user friendly system says more about our schools and colleges than simply their exam and assessment results. We hope also to have a fair and responsive complaints procedure which will provide us with valuable feedback on our performance.'

Improving the involvement of parents and the community is regarded as a major priority for the authority so that the public understand what the service at all levels is trying to achieve. Schools need to review parents' meetings, consider the introduction of parents' rooms and generally extend the access parents have to teachers: the views of pupils and parents need to be taken into account more. It is these values which establish the significance of establishing criteria for assessing and reporting on the performance of the education service to its public.

Performance indicators

Performance indicators are the lever for better practice by reflecting policies and clarifying how their progress is to be assessed. 'Performance indicators are statements, usually quantified, of resources employed, achievements secured and the intervening processes in areas relevant to the particular objectives of the enterprise.' The purpose of performance indicators is:

- to aid judgement and not to replace it;
- to complement the assessment of standards by involving the dimensions of progress and process;
- to provide schools, colleges and the authority with management information;

   – to assist in improving the effectiveness and efficiency of schools
     and colleges.

A bank of performance indicators is being established, some
of which will be core indicators to be applied to all schools,
while some will be chosen by schools to reflect evaluation of
their particular purposes. The process of clarifying the choice of
indicators will be part of the development planning process with
the advice of officers and advisers working in 'duos' in support
of schools. Indeed, the whole system of managing improved
performance and accountability in Warwickshire is to be supported
by a revised conception of organisational development: for the
department, the committee structure; and in a new governor
forum.

Organisational development

1. The department

Warwickshire, like many other LEAs, has felt the need to revise the
way they organise the department so as to reflect the changing role
of the authority in enabling local decision making while retaining
strategic leadership. An extensive consultation exercise took place
during 1989 on a new structure with the debate focusing firstly, on
the need for a clear definition of roles matched by a strong emphasis
on teamwork and partnerships and secondly, on the importance of
making decisions about the appropriate location for tasks/processes.
A new structure for the centre identified two branches to reflect the
principal functional responsibilities of the LEA post ERA:

Policy development and quality assurance divisions
These represent the emerging statutory role of the authority. This
ensures that the service is planned on the basis of more reliable
information, both in terms of performance and needs assessment.
Teachers and governors are encouraged to influence this part of
the authority's work through their contact with local inspectors and
officers in the areas.

Operational services and area offices
Through these, schools and colleges increasingly choose the type
and level of service required. Local inspector and officer teams
(LIOTS), the 'patch duo', together with the four area offices will

respond to requests for advice and support irrespective of any 'commercial' choices which institutions make.

The 'patch' approach to the monitoring and support of schools would involve 'duos' of officers and inspectors each responsible for groups of 15 to 18 schools and other schools sector establishments. The LIOTs reflect a growing awareness that in the new era, schools would require much more integrated advice and support than they have, hitherto, received from the LEA: 'we can't have one person talking about the curriculum and another talking about the budget'. Resourcing for example should reflect curricular objectives. The patch duo is the proper response of the LEA to these changing needs ensuring that officers and advisers work together to provide the appropriate advice to schools.

There are 23 'clusters' of schools and each will be served by a LIOT, a team of one officer and inspector. LIOTS will have committed time to devote to their cluster of schools, although they will have other responsibilities associated with their respective posts. How the team and the school make best use of the time available will be a matter for negotiation between them. LIOTS can provide information and advice; work with the school in its development planning; support the school in its self-review/monitoring process; relate this to the inspector's and officer's responsibility for monitoring, and evaluating and reporting on the work of the LEA's schools.

> We believe that the latter is best realised when the school takes on full responsibility for setting appropriate standards and targets and the LIOT needs to adopt a 'critical friend' stance and be able to report more publicly, as well as offer support.

Although the officers and advisers will tend to have their primary responsibilities, with the former concerned with curricular and pedagogic matters, and the latter focusing on financial, property and pupil role issues, nevertheless, it is expected that there should not be formal boundaries between the roles and substantial overlap if collaborative working is to succeed. Still less rivalry; the skills of officers and advisers are complementary and 'only through such partnerships will educational quality be defined and promoted'. The local inspector and officer teams will have meetings with local senior staff as well as the county education officer and deputy CEOs. It will be the responsibility of the chief inspector to evaluate the effectiveness of the LIOTS.

2. A new committee structure

A more streamlined committee structure has been introduced

from September 1990. Firstly, there are fewer members on the education committee, with teacher representatives no longer having a vote. Secondly, there is only one education sub-committee (performance review) to consider the performance of schools, colleges, community education, the department and county services to indicate the new policies and resource bids to take to full education committee. The performance review sub-committee 'emphasises the central importance of the LEA's post-ERA role', namely that of 'standard bearer of standards'. Thirdly, there will be only one members working party (strategy review). Simultaneously, there will be considerable streamlining of the 280 or so consultative groups, working groups and working parties. Many of these involved teachers, elected members, officers and inspectors.

3. A Warwickshire governors' forum

This forum is being established so that elected members and school governors can exchange views. At a local level one governor from each school in a cluster will go to consultation meetings. These will be twice a year. At county level each cluster will nominate three governors (primary, secondary and one other) to go to the twice yearly meetings of the Warwickshire governors' forum. The governors' forum meetings will discuss issues arising from the local cluster based meetings; report and discuss issues arising from education committee; and may occasionally have a key speaker on a topic of interest. The county forum meetings are to be administered by the governors' training unit, while the locally based meetings become the responsibility of the area education officers.

PART 2 1991–92

Charge capped

When the Secretary of State for the Environment published his list of local authorities to be charge capped for over spending it surprisingly included Conservative controlled Warwickshire. This was the cause of some anger in the authority because the previous year the budget had been deliberately kept low, in support of Government public spending policies, to ease the changeover from rates to the new community charge system. £5.6 m of service reductions were made then and reserves were drawn upon to keep poll tax bills down. The precept rose only 11 per cent compared with 17 per cent for similar authorities. Management consultants commended the authority on being 'one of the most efficient councils in Britain'.

Yet, paradoxically this cost cutting strategy has back-fired on the council in its preparations for the budget for 1991–92, penalised by its own restraint and the obscure controls on local government finance. The county argue that the illusion of spending increases derives not from local profligacy, but from the wholly inadequate and unfair standard spending assessment which fails to calculate accurately enough the spending needs of the council. Furthermore the county would have escaped capping if it had not made such large reductions in its precept the previous year.

The previous year's cuts left the council with an artificially low expenditure base (£250 m) with inescapable increases in expenditure (for example, to pay for statutory duties in relation to the national curriculum, rising rolls, local management formula protection) to be incurred during the year. Such spending increases would merely maintain the existing standards of service. But while the county council estimated that it needed to spend at least £285 m to maintain its services Whitehall estimated (the standard spending assessment) that Warwickshire should only spend £265 m (a 5 per cent increase producing a standard poll tax bill of £380) and would regard as excessive an increase in expenditure of more than 9 per cent above the 1990–91 level thus setting a 'cap' or limit on spending of £272 m. All spending beyond the SSA figure has to be paid for wholly by community charge payers and for every extra £1 m the Council spends above this level the poll tax payer has to pay an additional £2.75. Thus the cap level would mean a £19 increase in poll tax, while maintaining services at their present level would require increases in poll tax bills of £67. In this context, Warwickshire chose to set a precept of £278 m (virtually a 'standstill' budget with increases only to cover inflation while statutory commitments would have to be met by savings elsewhere in the budget), an increase of 11 per cent over 1990–91 although this involved painful cuts of £7.5 m in administration and services. In spite of these cuts the council was capped in March leaving it little time to find a further £6 m of cuts. Education had calculated that even without charge capping the service would need to find £8.4 m of cuts (including 25 per cent cut in the youth service and a 17 per cent reduction in the costs of administration) to pay for the inescapable commitments while protecting school and college budgets. Capping, however, meant a further £3.9 m cuts most of which (£3.2 m) would have to be borne by the general schools budget, including:

- 211 teaching posts would be threatened,
- primary class sizes would increase inexorably,
- there would be an increase in mixed age classes,
- a loss of teachers' non-contact preparation time; and
- the LEA's policy of providing additional teacher support
  to very small schools would have to be ended.

A capped budget, it was argued, 'would have a highly destabil-
ising and deleterious effect on the service as a whole' especially when added to the first effects of a move from an historic
curriculum-led staffing model budget towards full formula budgets
and the differential effects of incremental growth of school salaries'
commitment. The LEA believed that these financial constraints
would have:

> a dramatic effect on the capacity of schools to provide an adequate
> curriculum. This effect is variable, extending from schools with rising
> pupil rolls and/or who are 'winners' under formula funding to those
> which are 'losers' under formula funding and which may also have to
> lose funds because of an over estimate of pupil roll in 1990–91. In all
> cases however there is less money per pupil available in 1991–92.
> In 1990–91, the average cost per pupil in Warwickshire schools was
> £1,822, compared to £1,937 in . . . similar shire counties. In 1991–92
> the Warwickshire cost per pupil is likely to fall to £1,768 in real terms.
> The county's pupil/teacher ratio in 1989–90 was 21.0:1 (primary) and
> 14.6:1 (secondary). These ratios are likely to fall to 23.20:1 and 16.8:1, a
> change of 10 per cent and 15 per cent respectively. However the county
> average conceals enormous variations between schools.
> It is clear that in many schools it will not be possible to teach beyond
> a minimum level of National Curriculum requirements and, in some,
> this will be near impossible. The role of many headteachers will be
> to try and secure 'damage limitation' and developments relating to
> improving contact with parents, liaison with and fuller involvement
> of governors and regular support of classroom teachers (including
> the new appraisal system) will have to be delayed. For a significant
> number . . . of teachers and headteachers there is likely to be quite
> serious demoralisation and stress. None of this can be at no cost to
> pupils' achievement and behaviour.
>
> (Committee Paper, May 1991).

The LEA had already chosen to keep its public closely informed
and had produced, in January 1991, a helpful guide to the budget
preparations and the difficult choices implied. This was followed
by regular budget news updates. Full consultations were held with
schools and colleges in February in order to take into account
their views about which discretionary exceptions should, or should
not be delegated to schools. Every school was visited by their
officers/advisers (LIOT) support team. A governors' forum was

organised in March. This commitment to communication was more than amply rewarded.

When the capping was announced 'we were staggered at the local response' a senior officer commented. 26 petitions listing over 3,600 names, together with 1,738 letters were received, most protesting against the cuts. A deputation of 500 people went to Whitehall to deliver a 50,000 name petition while in Warwick 2,000 people including councillors, governors, teachers, and parents joined hands around Shire Hall as a gesture of unity against the cuts.

In the end a compromise was reached in May and the Secretary of State reduced the 'cap' by £3 m. The authority decided to give most of this benefit (£2.4 m) to education on the understanding that it all went to schools halving the loss of teaching posts. The chairman of the council as well as of the education committee believed that the compromise was hardly a victory and would leave education facing severe cuts that would cause the service to suffer. Charge capping has been a further burden upon schools:

> there's no avoiding over the last year, the overwhelming effect of charge-capping. There's also the move to formula funding which meant this Easter, that 25 per cent of the shift from historic to formula took place, and therefore, some schools suffered double jeopardy, they had to eventually take their share of charge-capping, but they also, in certain cases, had to take their first reduction from historic to formula, and I think also, schools have been overwhelmed in the case of primaries particularly, but to a lesser extent, secondary, by a sort of incessant stream of demands and changes in relation to the National Curriculum, and of course heads have more and more had to come through with the new kind of relationship with their governing bodies'.

Indeed the pressures of coping with contraction prevented both a number of schools and, in part the LEA itself, from introducing some of the strategies for improved management which the LEA was encouraging from the outset of implementing the Education Reform Act. Although, where those aspects of the new management were introduced successfully, schools and the authority were in a much more favourable position to manage change effectively.

Towards stronger management

The authority planned to phase the implementation of LMS to fifty schools at a time. But the success of the initial phase has meant that 'now everyone wants local management of schools tomorrow'. The schools have seen the benefits of having money in their own hands. An option of introducing LMS for all schools in April 1992 is being considered, even though enabling the creation of confident independent schools may 'set the seen for GMS'.

The process of implementing LMS has inevitably been a learning experience which has clarified how to strengthen the management of the service; in planning, rationalising responsibilities, especially in identifying essential information needs, and in managing quality.

(i) Strategic planning

The LEA made quite a lot of progress on strategic planning and being much more disciplined and precise about its role in establishing targets, certainly within the department, although less successfully in schools and colleges:

> we found that in the department, our development plan, which is expressed in terms of priorities and key tasks was an extremely important framework within which we set about making budgets cuts, basically, and that proved to be pretty resilient. It was also the case in about the 10 or 15 per cent of schools that had produced their own development plan, often with the assistance of officers or inspectors, that they found that the budget exercise was much easier, less traumatic certainly, because of that. But the vast majority of schools didn't have development plans. Some of them had development plans that were couched entirely in education and curricula terms, which harks back to another tradition and had not actually bothered to articulate their educational objectives with budget planning and budget management.

Preparing development plans was not conceived as being as high a priority as the National Curriculum, supporting governors, taking on LMS, as many of them have done this year. 'It's a victim of overload really'. Yet the experience of the budget may encourage more schools to produce development plans, although the new teacher appraisal system will require the introduction of such planning.

(ii) Reorganisation

The cuts led to a very large scale departmental reorganisation in the summer of 1990. Fifty posts were cut out and the numbers of divisions in the department reduced from 5 to 3. It has proved to be an appropriate structure in realising the LEA's broad aims while the division between services and strategic planning and quality assurance has proved to be a very effective structure. Furthermore the slimmed down education committee structure that was also introduced has proved to be very effective. Now, not as much officer time is taken up in preparing reports for committees or in sitting in working parties, but at the same time more effective reports have been produced. Undertaking such a major reorganisation of the officer structure illuminated obscure corners of administration:

> in setting up a new departmental structure, a great deal has surfaced there about the jobs people at lower levels have been doing, and for many years a lack of clear line accountability, management in other words, so that in corners in the department (and this applies to other departments in the council) people have been undertaking clerical tasks for which, as I said, there appears to be no current rhyme or reason, and I think within the department we've moved really quite strongly in the last year, and continue to move, towards a much stronger system of management, and we have in the department in the last year, now undertaken a staff appraisal scheme, which for over 400 people is quite something, and a great deal has emerged from that process in terms of a role and our function.

Yet, the LEA is beginning to experience a cycle of budgetary reduction leading to oganisational uncertainty and instability which can be counterproductive:

> people are feeling very uncertain, I mean I think they will be anyhow because we are in a very uncertain time, so they're quite right to feel uncertain, and one can help in that process to some degree and no more. The financial situation in the case of Warwickshire makes that even more difficult and we're finding it very hard to lop off functions and tasks, and my management team is having another go at it this next week because that's often the most difficult thing to do, to say, that if you've lost, as we have, 50 staff at senior levels as well as at clerical levels, what therefore, are the consequences for your priorities and key tasks. So we're having a day next week where we're going to look at all our priorities and key tasks and reduce them and put that to committee and say 'Look, come on, authorise this. Some things will have to stop!'

At the centre of the organisational development, and still requiring a great deal of 'matching and articulation' is a clear understanding on the part of all parties about respective roles and responsibilities between the authority and the individual school.

(iii) Information systems

One particular functional responsibility which has required developing is in monitoring and evaluating schools in order to report on their performance. The LEA believes it has been less effective than it should have been in working through, with schools particularly, their targets and the development of performance indicators. Yet exercising the function presupposes a reliable information system that provides for the needs of all the partners: it is properly regarded as one of the key conditions for school effectiveness.

Information has been identified as a serious issue at a corporate level throughout the authority. The management information required, for example, to monitor volatile (extra-authority) enrolment patterns in further education, or teacher absence and the cost of cover meant that the LEA was not able adequately to monitor its budget spend. 'We realised we lacked information systems, for example information on special needs for the LMS formula.' The information was not available to inform heads accurately about the implications of expenditure options for individual school budgets. 'We had global figures which could allow us to formlate global budgets. But we had never constructed individual cost-centre budgets. We could not do this at the same time as setting up the LMS system – the paradox is that the centre would have had to grow to enable this.' Working groups were set up within essential departments and within Education:

> to examine what the information needs were, what was required under statutory requirements and what also we thought we needed in order to carry out the authority's role. In the course of the last 6–8 months, a good deal of stripping out of information held in various forms and at various locations has been taking place. So really we've undertaken a very complex search in area offices within the education department, within headquarters, and also within other departments and have found a great deal of information which no-one is very clear about why we have it, I mean it's just dead, very much custom and practice emerging.

But a lot of other available data has been identified that could be assembled and used to evaluate performance.

(iv) Progress in the management of quality in schools

Senior inspectors are reporting that, probably, in about a quarter or a third of primary schools practice is improving as a result of the National Curriculum and the Standard assessment tasks. This is as a result of better quality materials, better quality objectives and programmes of study. There is also anxiety about the pressure placed upon teachers by the under resourcing of the reforms, and there is concern about the potential complacency in the secondary sector. Inevitably, it is regarded properly as too soon to make sound judgements.

> I think it's going to take such a long time to unfold that I think it's too soon to say. I mean certainly a lot of teachers are very tired, those that have been involved in the recent assessment, and such a lot has been done on the basis of voluntary cooperation and extra help and hours have been put in, but no system can continue on that kind of basis. Yet, I think in secondary schools, there's a rather worrying sense of things needn't change.

The more effective secondary schools have realised that there are enormous implications for their organisational structures, particularly any divide that exists between pastoral and academic or pastoral and curricula structures, and these schools are ahead of the game. They appreciate that issues such as assessment, reporting, and cross curricular themes cannot be managed adequately unless there is an integrated management approach. This points to merging the traditional separate management of the curriculum and pastoral systems. The LEA is looking to the inspectorate to report on this and to disseminate good practice or different models of good practice.

The work of the LIOTs has been valued by schools – though a survey of sixty schools has been undertaken to evaluate their work more systematically. Schools are now clear about their entitlement to LIOT support whereas in the past they may not have been visited by an inspector for two to three years. Yet the CEO does not believe that the system is strong enough to fulfil the expectations placed upon it. The inspectors are overstretched – for example 5 primary inspectors to cover 250 primary schools, and:

> I am rather worried, as I was last year, but even more so now, about the capacity of LIOTs to monitor and evaluate effectively, and to support management development in schools and including teacher appraisal, when the inspector concerned in LIOT is out of phase. In other words where you've got a primary inspector in a secondary school or to a lesser extent vice versa, and I'm just trying to work something out on that.

Growing understanding of the new roles

While the articulation of tasks and relationships between the LEA and its schools is taking time to develop, hindered by the cuts and the general climate of uncertainty, nevertheless a shared understanding of roles and a vision of public education is growing amongst the partners to the service. There is agreement about substantial delegation of resources to schools retaining perhaps 5 per cent of the general schools budget at the centre for strategic planning, for quality assurance and for networking, which is simply about, in the end, dissemination of good practice. Many share this view of the role of the education authority 'and an LEA could still have authority, and not simply be an administrative agency'.

This accord about the role of the LEA and its proper relationship with the partners has grown out of regular communication and meetings. It has come through the detail of the school circular, through countless meetings of heads or of teacher association representatives, and through the Warwickshire governors' forum. Senior management has learned 'to listen much more carefully, and picking up cues and signals whether from its governors or teachers or heads and so on'. The establishment of the educational development service, of the work of the advisory teachers and the teachers centre, has also encouraged a very clear sense of Warwickshire as a distinct kind of education authority with its own modus operandi. This unfolding corporate ethos across the Warwickshire education service may be influencing the attitude of schools to opting out.

Opting out

One school will become a grant-maintained school in September 1991. It had been proposed for closure by the LEA because it was believed to be educationally unviable. Two more schools, where parental ballots have voted in favour of opting out are now with the Secretary of State who is expected to approve them. A further school is organising a parental ballot. The motives for opting out include the search for a distinctive status as well as the wish to 'escape the full glare of public reporting' but the financial motive is believed to be significant ('the transitional grants are very tempting for two years'). Schools which have suffered from both cuts and the move from historic to formula budgeting have an understandable pressure to opt out. The allocation to GM schools of 16 per cent of the general schools budget to cover its purported proportion of central services is regarded by the authority as both an unreasonable incentive to schools and a regulation that is very likely to undermine the viability of the LEA:

> I think what hasn't been properly understood, and not just in Warwickshire, is that the 16 per cent rule that was introduced last winter means that – well it means two things at least. One is that an authority like Warwickshire, that wants to delegate more than 84 per cent can't because we'd end up double-funding any schools that opted out, but secondly that the actual effect of 16 per cent when it's secondary schools that are opting out, is now seen in other authorities such as Gloucestershire and Kent, where they've had quite a lot of schools opting out, to result in a need to reduce central services, inspection and so on by much more than 16 per cent, nearer 24–25 per cent, and that's because those central services are not actually used or needed on a pro-rata basis, and it's the primary schools that are having, if you like, more than their fair share of what that 16 per cent represents.

The 16 per cent procedure added to the other incentives and financial constraints is leading Warwickshire like a number of other LEAs to consider a number of strategies. The first is, with other counties to encourage members to lobby the Government about the incoherence and inequity of the regulation; the second strategy is to prepare literature which communicates openly and clearly with parents and the public about the implications of schools choosing GM status. One leaflet for parents called *Opting Out: Your Local Authority View* sets out the county's educational values; the attitudes of the LEA to opting out, and the county's decisions. Concerned to ensure that parents' and governors' voting is fully informed, the LEA has in 1991 prepared *Grant Maintained Status: The Facts* which describes the LEA's attitude to GMS; the legal basis of GMS; how GMS will affect the governors, staff and parents; what GMS will mean for the school's finances; why the local authority is needed, and who can give you advice. A third strategy is to consider an approach to retaining the collegiality of the LEA in the face of the new sector and thus undermine the debilitating consequences of the inexorable 'domino' effect of opting out.

> I mean I'm still thinking that if it goes on much further, all of this, that I'd suggest that all our schools opted out, because I don't think we can be responsible as an authority, particularly one that's charge-capped with meeting the requirements that Government has now placed on all schools. I mean in relation to the National Curriculum, local management or whatever it may be. We will simply reach a point, fairly soon, if say ten schools opted out, where we can no longer provide even at a minimal level, what schools need.

The LEA appreciates that the budgetary constraints together with its commitment to keeping schools fully informed, even about their entitlements under grant maintained status, may make opting out irresistable for schools. So the authority has introduced a consultation exercise with all schools, and governing bodies and staff, about 'a kind of associate membership scheme for grant maintained schools in Warwickshire, and the idea there is that, in a way, they'd be buying themselves back into the club, and there's a good deal of interest in that . . .' It's an expression of schools thinking 'Well perhaps in the future we may have to opt out. Maybe the Government will make us opt out or make it irresistible, or already we see the writing on the wall. But what we don't want is to lose what we believe the education authority represents'.

The details of the associate membership have still to be worked out. But the concern amongst officers as much as members, is that the creation of any such club would tend to be an administrative affair and what would tend to be lost would be the role of elected members and thus the institution of representative democracy. The county education officer in her speaking and writing believes it essential to the continuing quality of the service to develop understanding of the value of local democracy. Too often schools even 'have never been terribly aware or appreciative, indeed, of the role of elected members'.

Local democracy, it is argued brings a number of virtues to the education service: checks and balances in the use of power, redress against abuse of power, and responsiveness to the wishes of local people who have paid their taxes.

I think that in a major public service, paid for by and through people's taxes one way or another, either locally or nationally, there ought to be at local level an electoral system whereby people can hold to account their elected representatives for the quality of the services that they are paying for, that are their services. I also think at perhaps a secondary level – I'm not sure, when things go wrong and parents, or indeed staff, in or associated with the school want to appeal against what they believe to be an arbitrary or unfair decision, then that is also where a locally elected and locally accountable LEA has a very practical use, and I increasingly admire the way in which our committees actually work very hard to come to decisions which frankly a lot of people, whether heads or governors or politicians in London or bureaucrats in the DES would find extremely difficult to make, and it's really a very old principle of almost kind of '12 good men and true'. I don't know how you decide such weighty issues as the allocation of money to two schools, except of course, you could do it, I suppose, in London, but I don't think that would be as effective, and I think it's a question of where decisions are made most effectively.

The trend in Europe is to develop strong institutions of local government, based upon principles of subsidiarity and federalism, as the proper counter to the danger of excessive centralisation of power in society. 'I don't find many schools really believing that LMS in itself is a sufficient response to these kinds of constitutional issues: some do because they wish to when it suits them, but most in fact understand that we're talking about rather bigger and weightier issues than the self-managing school.'

The White Paper on education and training

In Warwickshire none of the political parties think very highly of the White Paper. It is perceived merely as an instrument to reduce local government expenditure and responsibilities. Senior officers do not believe that the technical problems of developing a national unit of resource for different programme weightings have been thought through. Objections have been lodged with the Secretary of State while the local TEC, it is claimed, do not welcome the imposition of new responsibilities and value their existing partnership with the LEA.

The LEA hopes that its 16–19 development fund, which straddles FE and sixth forms will be allowed to continue. Colleges and schools, it is argued, have said they would like this to happen, because of the evidence in the county of the way in which really quite modest pump-priming can make quite a difference to raising participation rates and broadening the curriculum and in improving progression, and these were the LEA's basic objectives when setting up that particular fund.

Conclusion

For Warwickshire the Education Reform Act has provided an opportunity to play a leading role in the creation of a service which provides high quality education and is more accountable to parents and the community. The reforms have provided an opportunity to examine critically the management and delivery of the service at every level. The role of the new LEA has been indispensable to realising the purposes of a more decentralised and responsive service. For without the strategic leadership which only the LEA can provide schools will not perform effectively, nor will the public be offered a service which is coherent and informed by shared local values. The authority has achieved a great deal: compliments have flowed from all parts of the service as well as from external observers about the quality of management and leadership in implementing the Education Reform Act. There have been a number of distinctive characteristics to the Warwickshire approach to the management of change in education:

1. Clarity of vision about how the service should develop in the new era informing a belief in the importance of strong leadership on values and policies from the centre. This has been a new experience for the education service in the county.
2. A system of strategic policy planning which provides both a sense of direction and coherence to the management of change. The system ties together the issues within education, ensuring that, for example, curriculum and resources are considered together, and also that the different parts of the service are drawn in, collaboratively, to this process of policy formulation: 'Policies were regarded as a nuisance in the past, and not possible in such a diverse county; yet without policies we felt the development work of the teams could not proceed. The team work requires a framework of clear values, purposes and policies'.

3. A commitment to partnership, that all parties to the service should feel that they belonged to and shared in its development. Partnership has implied a number of things:

   - Belonging: 'There has been a lot of talking to the partners, making the heads and governors want to be part of the club'.
   - Communication: partnership requires communication. Perhaps more than any other local authority, Warwickshire has values and invested in intensive communications with the service and the public. Through bulletins, booklets, newsheets, conferences, seminars and meetings, Warwickshire has sought to mediate and translate the extraordinary range of reforms contained in the legislation in guidelines to governors, schools and parents.
   - Participation and team work: partnership has meant an invitation to collaborative working, through project teams, meetings and working parties, teachers, advisers, governors and officers have worked together to plan, monitor and evaluate the changes.
   - Networking: providing support as well as information to the interdependent parts of the new system: offering a help-line to governors, and making regular visits to heads.

4. Style and culture: what the authority does is distinguished by style – that is not just in the distinctive image of all public communications, but more importantly the commitment to high quality of all that is done in the authority's name. A culture of excellence for public service permeates the work of the LEA.

The authority believes that the pace of change has not always been conducive to ensuring that the reforms are implemented with best interests of pupils and students in mind. Unreasonable pressure is applied. But the response of the partners has illustrated the quality of a public service.

Part 3 Towards the new local government of education

7
The LEA of the future

The Conservative Government's legislative programme, in particular the 1988 Education Reform Act has reconstituted the powers and duties of the parties to the government and management of education. It achieves this in a way that will create tensions for the LEA now caught between the markets of consumer choice and the hierarchies of Whitehall regulation of the National Curriculum. The legislation thus creates contradictions and yet possibilities for the local education authority. The four case studies have illustrated the responses of a number of local authorities to the education reforms which reflect their distinctive values and perspectives as well as shared understandings of the new management of education. This chapter seeks to review and analyse the discussion in the case studies in three parts: first, to consider the distinctive and shared values which LEA brought to bear from 1988 in reforming their management of education; second, to consider how they have confronted the increasing threat to the future of the LEA since 1990 constituted by the growing incidence of expenditure cuts, opting out and the take over of colleges propoposed in the White Paper on post-16 education and training; third, to develop the case for the indispensable role for the local government of education within a national partnership. The broader conception of the government of education is developed in the concluding chapter.

PART 1 FROM 1988: PERSPECTIVES ON THE NEW MANAGEMENT OF EDUCATION

While the Education Reform Act deprived LEAs of many of their former powers of control over schools and colleges it nevertheless accorded local authorities a significant strategic role in the reforms of education. As they set out in 1988 on the management of change what was distinctive and what common in the approach of the case study LEAs to their new role?

The distinctive perspectives of each LEA

Each of the four case study LEAs has developed a distinctive approach to the new management of education following the 1988 Education Reform Act. The perspective of each LEA, it will be argued, reflects values and assumptions, often implicit, about the nature of management. The LEA's approach will be discussed in turn.

Enfield anticipated early the trend in Government policy to create self-managing schools and believed that they would be vulnerable unless new forms of support were devised. What has been distinctive in the Enfield perspective is the idea that schools had to learn to collaborate and to support each other. Partnership was the key to the flourishing of education in the new era. If schools were to work together successfully to share resources and to plan the curriculum in order to maximise the opportunities for young people then they would have to learn to be more open with each other, to develop shared responsibilities and mutual respect. The barriers which schools often erect between each other that prevent the flow of ideas and skills would have to come down and this would require new confidence and trust.

The assumptions of management derive from a model of learning. Excellent management and excellent classroom practice are the same: openness to new experience and ideas; the capacity to revise knowledge and practice in the light of better understanding. Effective learning is actually more a collaborative rather than a solitary activity: ideas privately conceived need to be subjected to the sympathetic but critical gaze of others. Good managers work together rather than compete.

These assumptions define the management role of the new LEA. Their role is to enable rather than to control, to encourage institutions to work together and to provide them with advice and support. This requires the LEA to play a leading role in the strategic management of change: the LEA will be the catalyst to partnership, the guide into and through uncharted territory. The organisational arrangements of the LEA are conceived as a network of institutions and agencies as well as the department. The networking communicates images which fit the underlying philosophy of the LEA, that schools and colleges are parts of a whole yet possess their own integrity and autonomy so that relations between the parts are necessarily a matter of coordination. Authority within a network is negotiated rather than directed within a hierarchy of power. The constituent parts of the organisation are perceived as relatively equal bringing their distinctive specialisms to bear upon shared purposes. The department's enabling role is crucial yet nevertheless would continue to regard itself as *primus inter pares*.

Enfield has a sophisticated understanding of the necessary phases through which development takes place. The initial task was to establish the foundations for an effective education service by developing the infrastructure of resources and institutional arrangements. The next phase and continuing into the immediate future has been to develop the quality of professional relations and partnership. Though it is acknowledged that the quality of learning is enhanced when parents are directly involved it is believed that any extensive development in this direction should follow upon the successful accomplishment of the professional partnership. Increasingly, the LEA is conceiving a new role for itself as an advocate on behalf of clients and the public in relation to the service deliverers which might include parts of the authority itself as well as schools and colleges.

The distinctive approach of Kent has been to place *the customer at the centre* of the new management of education. The education service has to become much more responsive to the articulated needs and demands of its customers – referring in the first instance to schools and colleges, and then to parents and employers. The primary principle of Kent's management is 'closer to the customer' which means 'changing the focus of attention to the sharp end of the organisation where the relationship with our various customers takes place'. A customer oriented service will seek to clarify who the customers are, what they require from the service, what they say about us and, in response to such questions, the service asks what it can do to improve the service as well as make it more accessible and available. Customer care requires the service to be more open in dealing with its customers and be more willing to listen to their views.

The mission of serving the customer determined the style and process of managing education. Firstly, it placed quality at the forefront of service management because customers expect the highest standards or they will take their business elsewhere. Kent sought to pioneer a new approach to *quality assurance* that would provide a total quality programme to permeate the whole service, including financial matters as well as educational achievement. A set of performance indicators was being developed to support a more formal programme of school and college inspections. The approach is called quality assurance rather than control because the guiding principle is that quality of service is an attitude, rather than a technique, which derives from people who care and show commitment. Thus a process of self-evaluation will complement the more formal inspections. Much of the information about performance will be published in the public domain to demonstrate accountability to the public as well as to inform the choices of customers.

Secondly, the principle of closer to the customer implies much greater responsiveness of the service to customer demands and a capacity to provide them with the information they require. Customer care requires devolution of responsibility to give managers the discretion to respond flexibly to their needs. Devolved management means clarifying individual responsibilities and according them the resources necessary to fulfil their objectives but then holding them to account for the 'efficiency, effectiveness and economy' of their performance.

The principles of management which inform the Kent approach to the new management of excellence are those expressed *In Search of Excellence* (Peters and Waterman, 1981) that can be applied as effectively to the public as to the private sector. In a more competitive context excellent organisations are obsessed with quality in service to the customer. They encourage autonomy and entrepreneurship as the best way of developing good practice in response to customer needs.

The organisation is conceived as less tightly integrated than in the past. More of an 'association' to which members belong with the LEA adopting the role of the managing board of a company chain monitoring the quality of membership.

The management of the curriculum begins with the legislation and the National Curriculum but emphasises its place as one of the foundations together with the importance of 'areas of learning experience' and the necessity of schools taking into account their own experience. The world of industry and work is emphasised, but within a framework that is firmly committed to equal opportunities and the rights of pupils to a learning experience that supports their self dignity free from prejudice or discrimination. Active student centred strategies of teaching and learning are argued to be central to realising such objectives.

Kent's perception of the public is most in tune with the assumptions informing the Education Reform Act. That the public should be understood as meaning individual customers or consumers of a service whose active expression of choice is to be encouraged because of its significance for the effectiveness of institutions and the quality of learning.

The distinctive perspective being developed in Manchester proposed that the regeneration of the City and the educational underachievement of young people can only be accomplished by adopting radical policies of equal opportunities. Only when education eliminates practices which discriminate against students on grounds of gender or race or disability can barriers to achievement be dissolved enabling the potential of all to be developed and make its full contribution to the City. Equality of opportunity requires a new relationship with parents and the community so that the expressed needs of the public can influence the development of a service that can provide opportunities for all. Parents have rights as complementary educators to be involved in their child's development and need to be provided with opportunities to participate in classroom and school activities. For Manchester this understanding leads naturally into supporting the principle of teachers, parents, governors and the wider community working together in partnership to improve the effectiveness of education.

Manchester supports the delegating of responsibilities to governors and headteachers so that schools can respond more effectively to the needs of particular groups and communities. But the LEA is clear that delegation does not mean autonomy and that the quality of teaching and learning within the City will depend upon each part of the service perceiving their mutual dependence on shared commitment to values of equality and partnership. The LEA must become more proactive in developing policies with others to bring about the management of change. It must provide strategic leadership for the service.

Each new development of the service, whether it be the local management of schools, or the implementing of the National Curriculum, reflects the LEA's values of equality and public participation. The staffing decisions of governors must reflect the authority's equality codes of practice on recruitment and selection, while their decisions on the use of school premises must give priority, out of school hours, to community education. School development planning must demonstrate how the school is implementing equal opportunities and how parents are informed and involved.

The National Curriculum is believed to provide opportunities for schools, but is a minimum entitlement which has to be elaborated to meet the needs of a more culturally diverse community and to accommodate the experience which local knowledge alone can offer. Only this local interpretation and shaping of statutory requirement can enable all young people equally to develop their capacities. The Manchester curriculum is an equal opportunities curriculum preparing young people with the capacity for autonomy and responsibility to participate as citizens in the adult world. The learning environment should enhance the self-confidence of the pupil or student combating stereotypes and celebrating achievement. Manchester has promoted pupil profiling which accredits achievement so as to reinforce the motivation and qualities of all students.

The LEA believes that the monitoring and evaluation of the service's performance is central to its policy objectives. Only a broad audit of institutional development and of the service generally, supported by a comprehensive range of performance indicators can demonstrate the extent to which the aims of equality, of achievement, and of parental participation have been realised.

The distinctiveness of the Warwickshire approach is the commitment to strategic leadership of the new system of education. Whereas some other authorities have perceived a more detached enabling role for the LEA, Warwickshire has seized the initiative granted them in the legislation to lead the new local government of education. Rather than being undermined by the reforms, this authority perceives the opportunity to strengthen its role as the linch-pin of the new more loosely-coupled system. The LEA's traditional preoccupations with administrative detail was a distraction from what should have been its central function: the clarification and formulation of those values and strategic priorities that should shape the development of learning quality in schools and colleges that become more accountable to the public. When the LEA preoccupies itself with leading the service to agree shared values of learning quality then it is more likely to become much more effective in serving young people, parents and the community.

The new education service is understood not as a series of disaggregated institutions, loosely coordinated by a weakened LEA, but as an interdependent system in which each part has a distinctive role to play in the effective functioning of the whole. The distribution of powers and functions following the reforms reinforces rather than reduces the mutual dependence of the constituent parts – and central to any possible future coherence is the role which only the LEA can play of shaping and integrating the service. The indispensable process is that of strategic management: of determining purposes and policy priorities, programme planning and resource targeting, performance monitoring and evaluation, and reporting to the public. 'The authority's strategic role is a good example of the undoubted need to invent a local authority if one didn't already exist.'

The assumptions underlying Warwickshire's model of management are those of public service. The 'outputs' of the system are only effective or acceptable if the 'feedback' from parents and employers

demonstrates that they are happy with the service they experience.
The system must serve the public and learn from the public and if
it is to realise this aim it must learn to involve and work in new
ways with the public. This is the distinctive style and purpose of
the new management of education. Two concerns follow from this
preoccupation with public service.

The first is that it is the task of the LEA to ensure that the
education service is as much a local as national service. If the
learning needs of young people are to be met then the curriculum
has to be developed locally with the National Curriculum being
perceived as a set of guidelines for interpretation within each
community and within a distinctive LEA philosophy about teaching
and learning. In Warwickshire this means a commitment to an
education of the whole child through active and child centred
learning strategies.

The second implication of a public service orientation is a
commitment to quality and to developing systems of monitoring
and performance evaluation to ensure that the highest standards
of service are received by young people and their parents. In
Warwickshire, an 'early warning sytem' supported by performance
indicators is being developed to provide the service with the
necessary information for remedial action.

Organisational development is designed to support schools and
colleges in improving the quality and accountability of their service.
Local teams of officers and inspectors – indicating the growing
interdependence of these roles – will offer advice on development
planning as well as monitor and evaluate progress.

Each of the LEAs in this study has developed a distinctive
interpretation and emphasis to its programme of managing change
following the Education Reform Act. Yet, arguably, their strategies
for the new management had more in common than the distinctive
differences. It is to these shared understandings that the discussion
now turns.

Shared understandings of the new LEA

Although Enfield, Kent, Manchester and Warwickshire have developed their own distinctive approaches to the implementation o
the reforms of the 1988 Education Act, it is clear that the distinction
are ones of emphasis within shared assumptions about the purpose
role and management of the new local education authorities. Each
LEA would acknowledge the need for change within the loca
management of education and, while not agreeing with aspect
of the legislation, would accept that some reforms had merit anc

could be developed with benefit to the service. The authorities share a perspective that the reforms lay down a challenge for LEAs which, if taken up positively, can strengthen the local government of education. Whereas the traditional role of the LEA was to provide and maintain the administrative and institutional infrastructures for schools and colleges, now the overriding mission of the local education authority is to reform the process of learning, enhance the quality of achievement and promote a new relationship of service and accountability to the public. These values are complemented by a new understanding of management as strategic leadership of a service founded upon partnership. This vision of the new management of education can be encapsulated as follows:

1. A vision of learning quality and public service

The new management of education now centres upon interdependent values and purposes – equality of opportunity for all, the reform of learning, quality assurance and public service and accountability – underpinned by a commitment to strategic leadership and partnership. There is now a firm belief that if the quality and equality of education is to be transformed then a number of processes, which have in the past often been thought of as separate, need to be understood as overlapping and mutually reinforcing.

(i) From equal access to equal rights

Post-war education was committed in principle to equality of opportunity for all young people irrespective of their parents' wealth or power. The growing commitment to replacing selective with comprehensive schools greatly improved the access of pupils to educational opportunities. Yet the understanding of disadvantage (in society generally as well as the service) was often a limited one neglecting prejudices of gender and race that discriminated against the learning opportunities of girls and children from the black and ethnic minorities. Equal access to education needed to be complemented by equal rights to respect and opportunity within the learning process.

Whether in Labour Manchester or Conservative Kent, the new LEA is developing much more sensitive and assertive policies towards equal educational opportunities. It is now understood more clearly that unless the service carries equality of opportunity into the heart of the learning process then many young people will experience barriers to the full development of their capacities. In

Kent a charter of pupil rights set out their entitlement to expect cultural heritage to be valued, a learning environment free from prejudice and stereotyping, and a commitment of classroom and school to social justice. In Manchester dissolving discriminatory practices is regarded as the key to full equal opportunities. Enfield and Warwickshire are also committed to ensuring opportunities are provided equitably to meet the needs of all irrespective of gender, ethnicity, age or disability.

(ii) From providing resources to reforming the process of learning
In the past it was believed that the primary contribution of the LEA to curriculum development in schools and colleges was to improve the provision of resources; more teachers to improve the pupil teacher ratios or money for books and equipment were the best methods of helping pupils to achieve. LEAs developed advisory services of subject specialists who worked with teachers in their departments (in schools more than colleges) to improve the curriculum and teaching of their particular discipline. It took the developments of the 1970s to stimulate many LEAs into preparing curriculum policies for the authority as a whole.

Now the new LEA believes it should have a vital role in reforming outmoded conceptions of teaching and learning. Each of the LEAs is striving to work with teachers and other professionals to reform the process and content of the curriculum that enables a more active and flexible approach to learning. The aim is to encourage young people as well as adults to assume an active and responsible role within the learning process that will empower them with the capacities they will need to become creative participants within society. This forms the agenda of the 'resource based learning' approach in Enfield, 'active learning' in Manchester and Warwickshire, and 'investigative learning' in Kent. Realising these aims will require teachers, advisers and officers to reform the system of learning – the curriculum, the process of teaching, progression and continuity between the stages of learning, how learning will be assessed and reported, and the approach to counselling and care. Each of the case study LEAs has understood that if such a new paradigm is to be created the authority will need to have a clear vision of its own curriculum needs in order to interpret and shape how the National Curriculum is to be implemented and further developed. If the reforms to the quality of education are to be achieved then the LEA must play a leading role in transforming the system of learning. Indeed, for Enfield learning becomes both the end and the means of the authority: a 'learning service', one which continually opens itself to new understandings, is one most likely to improve the quality of achievement at all levels.

(iii) From input standards to learning quality

LEAs in the past would assess their progress in terms of standards of provision, on levels of expenditure and staffing ratios. The emphasis was upon provision for the service, upon inputs, on the assumption that given the right conditions, the appropriate infrastructure, then teachers would be able to apply their professional skills to the benefit of pupils and students. The LEA did not need to attend to the process or the outcomes of learning.

Now, the new LEA believes it must have a strategic role in assuring the *quality* of learning, identifying and disseminating good practice in curriculum development and teaching method; encouraging clear and consistent thinking throughout the service about educational values and purposes; making staff development suit the needs of institutions by encouraging good management; and, especially by developing a system of monitoring and evaluation that encourages schools and colleges to review their performance and complements this with processes of evaluation that assure the public of the quality of teaching and learning. The four LEAs are each developing new perspectives and systems to assure the quality of their service: Manchester is committed to a whole school audit approach to monitoring and evaluation, while the primary purpose in Kent is to develop a total quality programme which pervades the whole organisation; in Warwickshire 'the provision of high quality education is the glue that secures coherence, shared values and success' and Enfield builds in evaluation of performance to the centre of their planning process.

(iv) From service to clients to service for the public

A rejuvenated vision of public service informs the new management of education. In the past education, as much as other local authority services, emphasised the professional nature of their work in a way that placed the public in a client role to the authoritative judgements of teachers, advisers and officers. Professionals always conceived of their work as providing services *to* the public, believing they knew what the public wanted: now there is a growing realisation that in offering services *for* the public they do not always know best and need to listen to articulated need as well as negotiate priorities. There is now a revaluing of the necessary role of parents and communities within the process of learning as well as a new grasp of the proper accountability of professionals to the public within the public domain. Manchester promotes the rights of parents to be involved as partners in the service while Kent's mission is to put the customer first, listening to and providing services for the customer; Warwickshire strives to develop an education system which can learn from public feedback; and Enfield seeks to serve the needs of parents and the community. This new orientation to public service is based upon the growing belief that working more closely with parents and the public will help to improve the quality of learning while demonstrating the service's proper accountability.

2. The new management of education

The challenge for the LEA is to develop a capacity for management that can deliver this vision of learning quality and service to the public. Although each of the LEAs in this study may have begun to form a variety of approaches to management they nevertheless share a commitment to their role in leading the management of local education. This involves a statement about their relationship both with central government as well as their constituent schools. Each LEA is strongly committed to local government and to the view that a national education service does not entail 'local administration'. The quality of local education, it is argued, depends upon LEAs developing the capacity to clarify purposes and policies which respond to the needs of their local communities and the strategies which emerge from this process are used to interpret and mediate national policies emanating from Whitehall.

The LEA can make the new system work to the benefit of clients and customers, but it must assert itself to realise this end, and not only with civil servants but also in its relations with governors, heads and principals. Although schools and colleges are accorded new powers so that they become quasi-autonomous institutions within an LEA each of the LEAs in this study believes firmly that unless they perceive themselves as parts of an interdependent whole which is led by the LEA then the quality of education for all will founder. The challenge for the LEA is to assert a new style of leadership which wins the commitment and enthusiasm of schools and colleges to a shared agenda of reform and renewal of learning quality. The core values of the new management of education are: strategy, partnership, the enabling role, networking and public accountability.

(i) From adminstration to strategic management
LEAs typically interpreted responsibility for services as involving the need to administer their day-to-day operation, detailed decisions about staffing and finance were taken by the LEA sometimes to the exclusion of developing a clear sense of purpose, policy and strategy. Many LEAs welcome the devolving of administrative responsibilities since 1988 which has allowed them to focus upon the strategic direction of the service.

Now LEAs are clear that they can only lead the reform of local education if they can develop a process of strategic management which clarifies aims and priorities and programmes their implementation. Management is the process of choosing the direction of change. The cycle of strategic management might include developing:

- clear values and objectives;
- analysis of need;
- strategic priority and choice;
- a programme of action (a development plan) which identifies:

  – tasks; and
  – targets for completion;

- a budget plan defined by priorities and with resource targets;
- a programme of communication and staff development to support the strategy;
- a process of monitoring and evaluation.

At the same time as creating such a process of strategic policy planning at the level of the authority, the LEAs are encouraging schools to prepare their own development plans as a means of determining their own priorities and plans. The LEA strategic plan is conceived both as the framework to shape school level planning but also as being responsive to the needs and priorities which are articulated in their plans. If the LEA is to achieve any coherent sense of direction clearly it depends upon their capacity to work out with schools and colleges agreed purposes, priorities and plans.

(ii) From control to partnership
The post-war LEA had the formal powers to control its institutions and expressed values of professional expertise which placed their public in the subordinate role of client. Power lay with the LEA. The Reform Act has changed this, depriving the LEA of many of its traditional powers while enhancing its strategic responsibilities.
The response of many LEAs, as illustrated in this study, is to reconstitute the service around the principle of a partnership with governors, teachers, parents and the public. Enfield have built their new management around the theme of partnership:

> Partnership in many forms underpins the education service in Enfield where there is an emphasis on inter-dependence, shared responsibility and collective action. To be successful partnership needs to be based on mutual respect, a shared responsibility, and a wish to help others develop. This requires confidence and trust. To cooperate successfully schools need to be confident enough to have permeable boundaries. . .

The partnership scheme is intended to bring schools together in an organised, cooperative system which enables schools to support each other and the LEAs to support the schools.

Manchester has also founded its management upon a partnership which emphasises the home and community as much as the institution in working together to develop effective schools. Each of the LEAs believes that improving the quality of learning depends upon developing a new relationship with parents and the public. It is realised that the professional reforms to the process of learning need the confidence and support of parents and this requires LEAs, schools and colleges to find new ways of involving parents, employers, governors and the community as partners in education. Even HMI, the priesthood of professional educational knowledge increasingly urges schools to form a partnership with parents to improve the quality of education: 'schools are part of society and accountable for their performance'. Evidence of the benefit of involving parents and the community as 'complementary educators' is evolving in these LEAs as elsewhere: in nursery and infant classes, in primary home – school reading schemes, in secondary school tutor group parent associations and home – school councils, and in members of the community becoming 'coaches' to young adults making the transition from school to work. Through such strategies and many more, parents and the community improve their understanding of schools and their curricular aims. A shared mission is developing of the role of parents in the learning process and the need for schools, supported by the LEA, 'to reach out and support . . . parents' as 'partners in a shared task for the benefit of the child'.

(iii) From providing to enabling
The LEA was sometimes known as the 'providing authority' for its traditional role in administering the provision of educational services to a local area. These would include not only the phases of education but also the guidance services (for example, careers) as well as support services (for example, catering). Following the Reform Act, LEAs will be less preoccupied with the provision of services. The quasi autonomous nature of schools, colleges and institutes breaks the direct responsibility for provision. The role of the LEA will focus more upon offering advice and guidance to enable institutions to improve the quality of their services:

- governor information and training ;
- management advice (legal, personnel, organisational);
- financial planning;
- information systems;

- marketing;
- training;
- quality assurance.

The LEA shifts towards a role of support rather than control. LEAs will still offer services – on child guidance, careers advice, education welfare and so on – but increasingly their survival may depend upon the quality of service as perceived by the contracting institutions. The focus of advice changes. In the past advisers provided advice and support to teachers in their subject departments rather than to heads and the management of schools. Increasingly, as Kent recognise, the 'scope of advice and support will need to be enlarged, the diagnosis of educational problems must go deeper and the destination of advice and support will be more directed at heads, principals and particularly governing bodies.'

(iv) From informal to formal monitoring and evaluation of performance

The education service has always evaluated achievement, but its purpose and form has now changed quite radically. Evaluation, in the past has been typically informal and ad hoc. Such and such a teacher, or department (more often than the school) is 'good' another 'struggling'. Who or what was achieving or failing would form private understandings amongst advisers (more than officers) and teachers. Now there is a widespread belief that the evaluation of performance has to become a much more formal and systematic process which focuses upon the working of the institution as a whole.

The neglected role of quality assurance now comes to the fore as a principal function of the LEA. Each of the case study authorities is developing mechanisms for a more comprehensive and continuous monitoring and evaluation of the performance of educational institutions. LEAs are developing performance indicators on a wide range of practices and information systems to provide regular data on performance. The LEAs are clear that any monitoring and evaluation of performance must involve both internal processes of 'self-review' but also external processes of inspection so that quality assurance is linked to understanding of the learning process but also to public confidence and accountability. A whole school audit approach is regarded by Manchester as the most effective way of supporting equality of opportunity as well as the confidence of parents and the community.

(v) From professional dialogue to public accountability
The emphasis, in the past, upon professional expertise and judgement encouraged the belief that the development of the service
and its quality were a matter for the internal discussion of officers,
advisers and teachers. Now there is growing understanding and
acceptance that if education is a public service which is striving
to improve the quality of its achievement then it must find new
ways of working in partnership with and being accountable to the
public. For Warwickshire quality is the purpose of accountability the
mechanisms of which secure achievement and public confidence.

A number of strategies are being developed to improve the
management of accountability. The improved management of evaluation will provide information about the performance of the service
that can provide an early warning system for an LEA if necessary
to take remedial action. The LEAs in this study are committed to a
public system of reporting on a broad range of performance indicators
that can lead to an understanding of what the service is achieving
while revealing those points where action is required. Performance
indicators are regarded as providing necessary information for the
service and aids to judgement rather than arbitrary weapon to
replace it. Similarly, a complaints procedure for parents and students
is intended to establish opportunities for fair and open contact with
the service, encouraging informal liaison in the first instance.

(vi) From hierarchies to loose–tight networks
The organisational arrangements of the post-war LEA emphasised
the virtues of the 'segmented bureaucracy' with strong service
departments (primary, secondary, further, special needs and so on)
located within an administrative hierarchy led by the chief education
officer as head of profession. Education officers have been used to
working within an office that centralised administrative decision-
making while experiencing more discretion about professional
developments within each particular service sector.

Now new forms of organisational arrangement are being developed
which seek to devolve administrative decision-making to schools but
also to local areas, either to formally constituted local area offices or
to informally working networks of institutions working in partnership
to develop the curriculum and the resources which make it possible.
The new LEA will be more decentralised than before so that it can
become more responsive to the needs of schools and colleges but also
to the articulated needs of parents, employers and the community. At
the same time the LEA will be developing and centralising capacity
for strategic decision-making so that the authority can interpret the
diversity of 'voices' from the service and its public so as to clarify
strategic priorities and choices for the future direction of the service.

PART 2 FROM 1990: CONFRONTING THE THREAT TO THE LEA

While the 1988 Education Reform Act redefined the roles of the local education authority it appeared nevertheless to accord it a significant place in the new government and management of education. The case study LEAs all indicated their commitment to making the new system work although they each brought distinctive values and perspectives to create a new local management of education. Yet hardly had they begun in earnest the process of implementing change than a number of contradictory forces gathered momentum to threaten the creative innovations of these LEAs and potentially their future survival. In this section the discussion reviews how the LEAs responded to the pressures of cuts, opting out, and the White Paper by tightening their management and asserting their rationale. Yet the pressures threatened to undermine their distinctive achievements in constituting the new management and the conditions for its effectiveness.

Each of the LEAs has experienced cuts in expenditure which have threatened the integrity of their reform initiative. To avoid being charge capped Enfield was constrained to set its expenditure virtually at the standard spending assessment (SSA) imposed by central government. While negotiations with Whitehall about the validity of this assessment together with the Council's own prioritising of education to protect school budgets alleviated substantial teacher redundancies, nevertheless the reductions still required eroded the foundation of the LEA's approach to reform. The cuts to INSET and, in particular, the curriculum initiatives budget attacked the very conditions which made possible the operation of the partnership scheme and collaborative working between schools. The cuts have also threatened services, such as instrumental tuition, and eaten further into central administration that will require a formal reorganisation. In Kent, an authority which planned over time to augment its spending on education, the council has been driven to implement a massive programme of cuts which quite simply demolished the central component of its reform strategy – an ambitious, locally provided, quality assurance programme that would have enabled the routine monitoring and evaluation of all institutions in the county. That approach has had to be set aside in favour of a centrally administered sampling of inspections and an increasingly commercial organisation of advice and support. The careers, youth and community services have all received substantial cuts and awards have been reduced. £40 m of cuts in Manchester's educational expenditure have damaged initiatives which were perceived by many as key to the reform of educational quality in the City. The educational development service was dismantled while heavy cuts have been imposed on curriculum initiatives and in-service professional development. Although contraction may have improved the efficiency of further education, cuts to the adult, youth, museum and music services are regarded with less equanimity. While school budgets have been protected the continuing squeeze on central administration has required a further reorganisation. In Warwickshire, however, charge capping did have its impact on school budgets, teacher employment and class sizes.

There is, therefore, much continuity in these LEAs' experience of budgetary contraction. The cuts are increasingly forcing local councils to spend on education at the standard spending levels required by Whitehall. But these assessments will, it is clear, provide for a very limited, 'standard', service, one much below the quality expected even by the most prudent of local authorities. The cuts are having their primary impact upon those functions which the LEAs believe to be central to their strategic responsibilities; for example, quality assurance, or in enabling partnership through curriculum and professional development, or in providing services that support the special learning needs of the disadvantaged. The resources required to run the central administration are also now being reduced to a level below which the authorities would not be able to deliver their statutory responsibilities. Moreover, not only will this scale of contraction put non-statutory services, such as adult and youth services, at risk but the level of school budgets will also be diminished seriously. Enough to precipitate many schools to opt out. That is, of course, what many in local government now perceive to have been the Government's primary agenda and which presents a further and darker threat to the survival of the LEA.

The case studies offer interesting differences in opting out which need clarifying and interpreting. In two (metropolitan) LEAs no schools have yet begun proceedings to become grant maintained, while opting out has begun in the two county LEAs, one at an alarming rate. Thirty schools have begun procedures to opt out of Kent LEA although a small number have not been supported by parents and one has been rejected by the Secretary of State. Yet there is a trend towards opting out which, if it continues, accompanied by the financial regulations which require an LEA to allocate 16 per cent of its central administration budget to GM schools, then the authority will, as one officer anticipates 'go bankrupt'.

How are the different rates of opting out to be explained. Interpretation requires a theory which I have set out elsewhere (Ranson 1980, 1991). Integrated LEA systems, it is proposed, will survive the constraints as well as the pressures to engage in internal differentiation and competition better than fragmented systems. Opting out will, therefore, vary according to:

(a) Choices of the actors involved; their
   - values, is opting out valued or not?
     Is education conceived as a cooperative or competitive process?
   - interests, will opting out benefit a school financially?
(b) Constraints – what are the contextual pressures which the local system must confront: in particular:
   - surplus capacity of school buildings: which causes inefficient use of scarce resources, requires (ideally) the LEA to propose schemes of school closure yet this is likely to precipitate opt out proposals. This dilemma is further accentuated by the understanding that spare places in the system also increase the possibility of parental choice and thus competition between schools for pupils;
   - LEA budgetary contraction: the greater the cuts imposed on local authorities, the greater the risk to school budgets and this increases the interests of governors and heads to propose an opt out ballot.
(c) Structural characteristics of the educational system: integration will vary with:
   - institutional characteristics: those systems are more vulnerable to internal competition and opting out which are differentiated:
   - horizontally: the proximity of different kinds of school system: for example, 11–14, 11–16 and 11–18;
   - vertically: selective systems which constitute a hierarchical ordering of academic status;
   - characteristics of managing the system: is the system organised as an integrated, interdependent whole, or is the system regarded as one of loosely connected parts administered by the LEA? The latter will be more vulnerable to differentiation and opting out.
     The greater commitment to the local management of schools – delegating more money to the potential schools budget (PSB), and to more schools over a shorter period of time – has the potential to encourage more competition between schools. Although there is nothing intrinsically competitive about LMS this Government's gearing of the formulae is in effect a voucher scheme designed to reinforce the accumulation of pupil numbers;
   - cultural characteristics: do the traditions of the system

encourage partnership and collaborative working or relative autonomy and competition? The latter will be more vulnerable to opting out.

There are therefore a number of dimensions which need to be taken into account in order to produce any adequate explanation of opting out. Social forms are not determined but largely shaped by the choices of dominant groups within the system. Yet these groups do not exist in a vacuum and are always located within, and limited by, some contextual and organisational constraints. The pace of development will depend upon the mediating structural conditions outlined in the theoretical framework. How do the case studies test the theory?

Although the study, at this stage of the research, has not focused upon schools, it may be reasonable to hypothesise that at least some heads, governors and parents have *valued* the creation of a grant maintained sector together with its rationale in strengthening institutional autonomy from local government as well as the purported growth of parental influence. Some of the proposals to opt out, for example in Kent may have had their source in such values. It is clear however that none of the LEAs in the study has supported opting out although councillors in Kent have been constrained to adjust their initial hostility to a more neutral attitude of willingness to trade – without which their survival would be at risk. The interpretation of the balance of interests involved is more complicated. If an unknown number of schools might value opting out it would seem clear that it would be in the interests of many more, in a short term calculation of material advantage, to opt out either for survival or financial benefit. And, indeed, all the evidence from these LEAs is that the contextual constraints have tipped the balance of interest for a number of institutions towards opting out.

While the urban authorities, Enfield and Manchester, had reorganised their schools in the 1980s, thus approaching the ERA reforms both from a basis of stability and more significantly without the surplus capacity in schools which can encourage competition, both the counties however, especially Kent, have recently introduced schemes of institutional rationalisation. A number of the proposals have threatened schools with closure and they have responded with proposals to seek grant maintained status which the government has acceded to (thus causing confusion within the LEAs which believed that institutional rationalisation was one of the Government's policies).

While a number of the initial applications to achieve grant maintained status have, therefore, been caused by schools striving for survival in the face of schemes of reorganisation proposed by LEAs in order to make their services more efficient, the evidence grows, in the case study authorities as elsewhere that the drift to opting out is motivated more seriously by the growing financial constraints placed upon local authorities and the long period of underfunding education. Reinforced, of course, by the considerable financial incentives (capital as well as revenue) dangled by Whitehall to entice schools away from their local authorities.

The impact exerted by the constraints and the influence of the incentives depend however upon characteristics internal to the LEA system – in particular, the extent of integration and the value accorded to cohesion – as much as the constraints facing the LEA. While Enfield and Manchester have integrated institutional systems there is greater diversity to those in Warwickshire and Kent which incorporate, especially in the latter, selective schools that create a hierarchical order of academic esteem. In Kent the policy of eliminating selection at 13 plus is intended to ensure conditions of LMS equity between schools. Officers anticipate that rivalry between high schools and grammar schools will be accentuated as they compete for 'upper band' pupils and that some of the smaller grammar schools may go under. In this context, grant maintained status with its privileged resourcing is clearly in the interests of vulnerable schools selective or otherwise. Kent is a fine example of institutional systems containing within themselves the conditions for their own disintegration.

Whether differentiated institutional systems are vulnerable to fragmentation depends, however, upon characteristics of the management process within an LEA as well as cultural traditions. Warwickshire, for example, has a variety of institutions some of which are selective and a tradition of relative autonomy from County Hall, but the qualities of strategic leadership and the policy of partnership in the implementation of the Education Reform Act have, it appears, been valued by schools and the collaborative response of all the education partners to charge capping indicates the development of a more cohesive service than the county has known hitherto. The lack of opting out in Manchester and Enfield can be attributed to a great extent to the culture of partnership between the authority and its schools in the management of change. In Kent the authority has tackled with consummate skill the challenge of establishing the conditions for managing a new and more effective customer oriented service, yet this requires a timespan which is no longer available to it – the same objective has taken Enfield, for example, over a decade to accomplish with proficiency.

While it seems that the trends to opting out in the four case study LEAs have not been 'chosen' by the local authorities, or the main body of governors, head and parents, they are nevertheless the outcome of an interplay of forces which could have been predicted and thus intended. The dominant player in the game is undoubtedly central government constituting the rules of play and fixing the rates of exchange to determine its preferred outcomes. The Education Reform Act was, it can be argued, always designed to constitute educational markets that would weaken the dominance of planned systems and strengthen the growth of autonomous and competing institutions. In spite of understandable scepticism about whether the inducements to schools will continue over time once a threshold of schools opting out has been reached, there is resignation in each of the four LEAs that another Conservative Government will cause an acceleration of opting out; the drift will become a flood. While this may remain a probability, not least because of the prospect of further legislation required to sort out a policy which is in danger of causing as much turmoil in Whitehall as it is in town or county hall, nevertheless the above analysis suggests it is not a certain outcome. The commitment, of parents (purportedly) as much as the professionals, to collaborative working amongst the partners may resist the entreaties of underhand government. Indeed, in three of these LEAs the strategy is being contemplated of encouraging all to opt out simultaneously and rejoin the LEA in the form of a voluntary association. If the LEA had not existed it would need to be invented.

The discussion in the opening chapters illustrated that the Government was not much interested in inventing local government. Rather the reverse. While expenditure contraction and opting out seem designed to erode the conditions for the local government of education, the White Paper on education and training will confiscate institutions that are central to its functioning. The LEAs resent the assumption that they have not been committed to the reforms described and the ommission of their role in creative innovation. Furthermore, the proposals are dismissed for their failure to develop a radical perspective on integrating post-16 education and training, and their muddled analysis in failing to grasp the significance of colleges as an indispensable local resource in such a system.

The response of the LEAs to financial contraction has been to intensify the processes already underway in the implementation of LMS to create a tighter and leaner framework of management. A commitment to teamwork within the department and partnership with schools has served to clarify a shared understanding of new roles and relationships. The LEA has worked hard at developing accurate and efficient systems of information and finance which provide schools with the advice and support they demand.

Yet the LEAs understand that what is at issue at the present time is not really the efficiency of their management, however important they acknowledge that to be. Rather it is the fundamental question about their rationale and whether they should exist at all. They have begun to prepare papers, to meet privately as well as speak and write publicly about the significance of local government in and for education. Because without agreement about the existence and role of the local education authority the very conditions for an effective management of change cannot be provided by elected members and officers. It is to these arguments – to the case for local government of education – that the discussion now turns.

PART 3 THE CASE FOR THE LOCAL GOVERNMENT OF EDUCATION

The radical agenda of the 1988 Education Reform Act has been to improve standards of achievement, the quality of local management, and to bring about better accountability linked to a more informed parent body. The reforms to the government of education left the role of the local education authority in an ambivalent position, bereft of many of its former powers yet provided with an opportunity to develop a strategic role at the centre of learning quality. The case studies in this book illustrate, I believe, the imaginative and essential contribution being developed by local government to the national education reform movement. Nevertheless, the future of local government in education continues to remain uncertain as the discussion of government attitudes and policy in the opening chapters revealed. Other commentators (O'Connor 1990) and academics (Hargreaves 1990) have proclaimed the LEA redundant in favour of a regional tier or a consortium of schools taking over the functions of local government. Yet this study, it can be argued, provides evidence to support the belief that the contribution of the local government of education is indispensable if the aims of the legislation, or indeed any reforms of learning quality, are to be realised.

Any analysis of the case for local government in education needs to sort out a number of issues which are often overlaid in the critique of local education authorities. The case for local government depends upon winning three arguments:

1. that education is inescapably a system, locally as much as nationally, that must have an integrity geographically as well as in terms of the interdependence of related services if the service is to fulfil purposes of equality and quality in learning;

2. that education must be regarded as a local, as well as a national system, if the service is to fulfil its purposes of equality and quality in learning;
3. that the local system must be democratic rather than merely administrative, if the service is to fulfil purposes of equality and quality in learning.

These arguments will be considered in turn.

1. The systems of education

The conditions for learning lie beyond as well as within the boundaries of the self. Unless learning is supported in the home, the school and the wider locality, then many may be left without the motivation to learn. Learning requires wider communities of learning as well as the learning institution. The layers of the whole need to be mutually supporting if the potential of each individual is to flourish. Institutional frameworks with responsibility for the wider contexts within which we all must live are, therefore, as vital for our well-being as those that we experience directly.

The local authority, it is argued here, has a pre-eminent role to play in these processes at a number of interdependent levels in local education; firstly, in developing the system of learning, secondly, in the system of local management and, thirdly it will be argued in due course that the local authority has an inescapable role in the public domain.

(i) The local authority in the system of learning
The art of pedagogy is neither transparent nor unchanging. Which processes of teaching provide supportive and stimulating contexts for learning, by generating the necessary self-confidence and motivation for young people to commit their energies to developing their intellectual and creative capacities, are grasped uneasily over time even by the best teachers and schools. Cultures of learning change over time and understanding the new codes into motivating the young and dispossessed have continually to be thought out individually but also collectively within and beyond each school.

Learning, moreover, is a process which cannot be contained within the boundaries of any one institution. Discovery and understanding occur at home, in the community, on a scheme of work experience as well as in school or college. The task of the formal institution is often to encourage reflection upon and interpretation of such disparate experience within processes of learning that are coherent and enable progress to be made from stage to stage. The

LEA has a pre-eminent role in promoting and enabling the quality of these processes of learning by:

- encouraging clear and consistent thinking throughout the service about the values of opportunity for all and the strategies of active learning to empower those who have been subject to social disadvantage and discrimination;
- developing the curriculum within the national framework to ensure pupils a learning experience which is broad and balanced, coherent, relevant and organised to allow continuity in learning across the curriculum as well as from stage to stage;
- developing progression between the stages of learning especially between primary and secondary as well as between 14 and 19;
- identifying and disseminating good practice in the learning process and in the achievements of schools and colleges.

The LEA has therefore a leading role to play in generating understanding of and the conditions for processes of learning which enable young people with a variety of needs to develop their capacities. The LEA is not only vital to the very conception of what quality and equality in learning is, but also to the means of creating the skills and understanding of the new culture within the service as a whole. The key to the success of reforming the learning process in the case study authorities, for example, in Enfield, lies in the partnership which has been created between teachers, advisors and officers to enable curriculum development, encourage new approaches to teaching and learning, as well as to plan programmes of professional development for teachers and staff.

If the reforms are to be sustained the LEA will become the necessary linchpin in partnerships between the profession, teacher (and curriculum support) centres, and higher education, clarifying staff development needs and how the providers are to make their appropriate contributions. The LEA in many areas is at the centre of innovation in professional development, encouraging providers to create more flexible courses and processes of accreditation which relate training to the needs of the school as much as the individual teacher. Moreover this development work is accomplished at a lower cost than could be achieved by institutions acting independently.

(ii) The LEA in the system of local management
The quality of learning depends upon the system within which it is located and getting the characteristics of the system right is a specialist function of government rather than a providing institution. If each young person is to make progress in their

education many organisations and agencies must work together rather than separately and this is the leading responsibility of the LEA. If schools are to cooperate in sharing resources and in developing the curriculum to improve learning opportunities then they need the support of an authority to create a new climate of trust and confidence. The new partnership in learning will not happen without the strategic leadership of the local government of education. Its indispensable functions and management tasks are to enable:

- A vision of local education that will shape the development of a system devoted to the learning opportunities of all, and which grows out of an assessment of what pupils and students need as well as from what parents, employers and the community expect from the service.
- Partnership, for if a coherent strategy for the service is to emerge it will require institutions and governors as well as parents and employers to work with the LEA as partners in a shared enterprise.
- Efficient provision if young people, their parents and schools are to experience a number of services. Economies of scale suggest that the inspite of delegation, the LEA will continue to have an essential role in ensuring that a number of specialist services are provided; to ensure that young people are entitled to a curriculum that enables access to potential minority subjects such as music and to ensure the provision of a wide range of specialist services affecting individual children such as child guidance, education welfare, careers guidance, support for special educational needs, assistance in transport and financial support where necessary. A number of non-statutory educational services, which are not peripheral but are integral to the health of 'mainstream' education, such as youth, adult and community education – will not flourish without the support of the local authority.
- Support to institutions: the LEA will be needed to pro-vide specialist advice on a number of financial, legal, and personnel matters to support schools and colleges in their management development.
- Planning and coordination: there is a need, for example, to plan the number of school places in relation to demographic changes, identifying the case for a new school or for closure and amalgamation. This process is best undertaken locally because of the need to understand and plan the system of learning as a whole.
  A system of schools which, for example, is suffering falling

rolls where numbers are declining unevenly and may change randomly, would be certain to suffer an effect in the quality of learning in all its individual schools. The changing numbers will have an effect upon the staffing and resources and thus upon the curriculum offered, while the uncertainty will effect the morale of teachers and pupils alike: the ethos (the climate of confidence and expectations) of a school cannot avoid being affected and perhaps undermined. In their study of *Falling School Rolls in Secondary Schools* (Briault and Smith, 1980) argued for an understanding of the delicate balance between the qualities which make a good school and the conditions necessary at the LEA level for providing them; the needs of the system and the insitution have to be in balance:

> There is a complex interaction between LEA policies, arrange-
> ments and provision of resources on the one hand and the policies
> and school management decisions on the other

The quality of learning in any one institution depends upon characteristics which have to be managed at the level of the system as a whole; the appropriate numbers of pupils which permits margins of accommodation that prevents congestion and facilitates movement and timetabling; the balance in the curriculum with choices at key stages which enable progression and provide for the growing diversity of needs; the right number of teachers appropriately trained with their committment sustained by programmes of professional development; and an efficient allocation of resources in relation to the social context of learning. If the schools are to remain comprehensive, then the intake to a few schools should not be allowed to become selective so as to create an imbalance in the remaining institutions. Unless the LEA manages the system as a system then the quality of learning within each institution is in danger of being diminished.

Local education is increasingly a 'tightly-coupled system'. The phases of education need to be planned together if progression in learning is to be maintained. 14–18 year olds, for example, whose learning needs increasingly straddle reflection and experience, require a system of education which embraces the world of work and life in the community as well as secondary and further education. Any adequate provision for those with special educational needs will require an integrated response from specialist institutions as well as those in the mainstream and this can only, realistically be coordinated by the LEA.

 — Evaluating quality: quality is necessarily a public rather than a
    private concept; what counts as standards of achievement or
    performance needs to be agreed locally as well as nationally
    and the LEA has an inescapable role in enabling the partners
    to agree a set of indicators which will define levels of expected
    performance. Through supported self-evaluation as well as
    inspection the LEA will have a strategic role in assuring the
    quality of the local education service.

The quality of learning in any one institution, it is being argued,
depends on the quality of the local educational system. One
element in the system cannot be treated in isolation from another
if each is to contribute to the effective working of the whole.
Teachers, the curriculum, resources and institutional forms are
interdependent and if their relationships are to be mutually beneficial the system needs to be managed as such. A mere consortia
of schools would be inadequate to the task. While the form of
management exercised by the local education authority requires to
be very different from the past as the case study authorities illustrate,
nevertheless, as each of them would argue from their different
experience and perspective, their contribution to the quality of the
new local management of education is indispensable for its effective
working.

Before proceeding to discuss the role of the LEA in the local
political system I want to consider the argument that the quality of
the education system described so far does not depend upon a local
education authority but could be better managed from the centre or
a regional tier of government.

2. A local system

If the argument so far has established the significance of the wider
system to the quality of education within any one institution it has
also implicitly argued that it is crucially a local as well as a national
system. While education should entitle students to a common
national curriculum it needs, if it is to be effective, to enable
young people to engage with the languages and cultures of their
local communities. The abstract principles of the national schema
have to be connected to and grow out of local experience and this
can only be accomplished through a local system which encourages
the partners working together to develop a shared understanding
of how local purposes can be expressed and be consistent with
national objectives. The case for the local development of the
curriculum and of innovative approaches to teaching and learning
was argued cogently by Enfield's CEO:

It is not to say that the National Curriculum doesn't have a place as a framework, but as a broad framework. But it is because you need a notion of constant evolutionary development of the curriculum and of education you then also need to have local curriculum development. . . To be effective the curriculum has to be continually renewed if it is to meet new local needs . . . local curriculum development has to come back again.

Furthermore, only a local process can manage the system with economy and effectiveness. Delegation to institutions has proved a major advance but the quality of local management, it is clear, also requires a tier of management, which is close enough to those schools and colleges to provide them with the appropriate advice and cost-effective services. A national or regional framework of administration would almost certainly be more remote from local institutions, less sensitive to their needs and less flexible in responding with the support they require. The strategic development and coordination of such services and support is best done locally because only then can the local partners be involved together and regularly enough to influence the making of decisions which effect their interests as well as the nature of the overall system.

In a changing, uncertain, society it is a local authority which provides the institutional conditions for responding to the diversity as well as the universality of learning needs. As Stewart (1983, 1984, 1989) has argued:

A local authority lies close to the area it governs. Decisions are made about situations known or seen. There is a possibility of responsiveness to local circumstances that is not open to the decision-makers at the level of central government, where decisions have to be made abstracted from local circumstances in the safety of a file. There is a capacity at local level for a style of governing less dependent on the uniformity of large rule bound organisations. In that responsiveness the learning can be grounded in local communities.

(1984)

A public education service, concurs the Society of Education Officers in a recent statement (June 1991), requires clear decision-making structures which exhibit the following characteristics:

- local, to ensure understanding of local needs,
- responsive, to achieve a high level of customer satisfaction;
- enabling, to give freedom to self managing governing bodies;
- large, to benefit from economies of scale in the operation of efficient support services;
- skilled, to facilitate effective decision-making locally, and reduce the need for national bureaucracy; and

    − which cover geographical areas and posses historical traditions with which local people can identify.

If the Society's proposals concluded at this point they would remain ambivalent. Indeed, such an ambivalence sometimes characterises the generalised criticisms, set out in the opening chapters, against local education authorities. The argument for local administration may in the end, one believes, be conceded, albeit as a residual institution, but not the case for local democracy. Some might like to retain the administrators but ditch the politicians. The SEO (as much as the case study LEAs), however, is quite clear about 'the importance of retaining local democratic accountability in the delivery of a service which must remain essentially local in character'. If the system of learning and the local system of management are to be effective they must be located within and underwritten by a system of local democracy and government as the defining characteristics of the public domain. Education is not a technical issue which can be considered apart from the debates which characterise the local as well as the national polity.

3. A system of local government

The quality of learning, therefore, is not only dependent upon the effectiveness of the local system of management, but crucially upon the wider local political system in which it is located. Learning quality, it is increasingly proposed, also depends upon the quality of public participation, choice and accountability. The importance of involving parents and community derives from a number of arguments:

    − involvement enhances the learning of their children;
    − to develop understanding;
    − their rights;
    − the rights to express views about education;
    − the need for local public choice;
    − the need for local democracy.

Parents need to be closely involved with schools working in partnership with teachers to support the learning process. The evidence suggests that where this happens the motivation of young people is considerably enhanced and this leads to significant improvement in achievement. The LEA has a crucial role in developing policies on the necessity of parental participation, and then in identifying and communicating good practice.

    It is, in part, because parents are so significant an influence upon the quality of achievement that the LEA together with schools need to reach out to develop their understanding of the many and varied innovations in curriculum and teaching over recent years. If parents are to fulfil their appropriate role as complementary educators then they need to make sense of learning strategies and this requires professionals to learn to work in partnership with parents, governors and the community. The LEA has once more a strategic role to play in this process. While professionals need to learn to communicate the meaning and purpose of new practice, they also need to listen. The best teachers know that by working with and listening to parents they can develop understanding of language and culture that can provide the key to the progress of particular pupils.

This significance of parents to learning, however, illustrates the necessary rights of parents to be involved in the school and the education system. Parents have a right to be:

- valued;
- informed about the school and their child's achievement;
- involved in decisions about their child's education;
- involved in school activities;
- involved in the learning process as complementary educators.

The participation of parents, many believe, can help break the cycle of underachievement in education. Such a defining characteristic of learning quality cannot be left to chance or to the insight of leading practitioners. If it is to define the quality of the system as a whole it can only be promoted across the service by the LEA.

The argument so far supports the participation of parents as individual consumers of the education service because of the direct benefit which this has upon their child's progress and their rights to become involved more generally because of their role as complementary educators. Yet education is a public good as well as a private benefit. Even if learning is considered an experience of individuals alone, in its influence upon character as well as 'skills' the education service will always have a wider significance which properly concerns the whole community as well as the individual attending an institution of learning. But to think of education as an individual experience alone or as the possession of institutions is, of course, an unduly narrow vision (which the ERA and the White Paper are in danger of expressing) of a service whose distinctive challenge, as we face the turn of the 21st century, is to enable the learning society (at work and home, or in the community rediscovering the traditions of an age past – of literary and mechanics institutes, reading rooms and discussion groups and learning cooperatives). The need to develop the community as a ıole as much as the powers and capacities of each properly makes education a service of and for the common wealth. It is this inescapable characteristic of the service which requires the participation of the public as citizens as well as clients and customers. Thus, people need to be involved collectively as well as individually in influencing the development of what is essentially a public service, the characteristics of which cannot be determined by individuals acting in isolation from each other. The quality of education therefore requires to be the subject of public choice which is accountable to the public as a whole.

If choice is to be public choice it requires the opportunity for citizens to express their view, for their voice to be heard, so that the inescapably diverse constituencies of education are enabled to present, discuss and negotiate their account. Public choice presupposes public participation and mutual accountability (Ranson 1989, 1990).

Such an active citizenship requires the necessary conditions for participation; extensive consultation and the use of surveys as well as using the authority's outreach staff to listen to the views of the public. Community polling could be another approach to encouraging public choice.

A constitutive condition, however, for any citizenship is to provide arenas for active public participation. A model in the recent past has been the creation of local youth councils which have enabled young people to debate and make decisions about youth policy and provision. Some schools have developed community councils which involve a broader representation than formal governing bodies in order to make the life of the school wherever possible serve the needs of the community as a whole as well as parents. Some colleges have sought to play an enabling role with community businesses by providing the community with skills, advice and resources to deploy as they choose. The role of the educator is to encourage community groups to take responsibility and ownership for their own learning enterprise.

An education service which seeks actively to involve citizens in policy making and become accountable to the community as a whole needs to constitute local community forums or councils. These would enable several interests – including women's groups, the black and ethnic minorities and the disabled – within a community to participate, articulate needs and contribute to decision-making. Where an authority has formed a pool of resources, perhaps from urban aid funds, EEC or local grants, to support community groups, decision-making about distribution could be delegated to these forums. In this way citizens within the community are being enfranchised to influence and take responsibility for their own learning environment. They can negotiate with the providers to use educational resources so as to meet the learning needs of the community as a whole: in 'access' courses, 'women back to work' classes, health courses, community languages and bilingual learning and so on.

Yet these developments presuppose the prior existence and pre-eminent significance of local government in and for education. Such initiatives to extend and improve participation of citizens in public services build upon and require the institutions of local democracy. Participation is needed to complement representation in the evolution of local government. The more immediate arenas of personal participation need to be underwritten and informed by the institutions and legitimacy of the council chamber and its public committees. In this way a more elaborate political system is developed which enables a wider public debate about the purpose and process of education, about

– the learning needs of individuals and groups;
– the rights and entitlements of the disadvantaged;
– complaints and injustice;
– ideas for improving the quality of service delivery.

Such a system would encourage public choices which were more responsive to the community as a whole and thus based upon consent and, at the same time hold services more accountable to the public (Bogdanor 1991).

The local education authority, therefore, is an institution of local democracy as well as a framework for managing the system to enhance the quality of learning. Its essential purpose, as well as its capacity to enable educational achievement, derives from this source. By unfolding capacities for responsible autonomy and choice an education generates the value as well as the conditions for living in a democracy, while an accountable democracy, through its traditions of public discourse, is the only means of ensuring an education worth having. Education and local democracy are thus mutually reinforcing; their purpose is one and the same – a learning society.

The functions of the local government of education have to be clarified in this context. The tasks of the LEA are in the end not merely to enable the new local management of institutions but the new local democracy of the learning society. The LEA, therefore, necessarily has a major role to play in developing the partnership with a more active public which is the fundamental condition for realising the vision of quality in public education that lies at the centre of the 1988 Education Reform Act. For some (Maden 1990, Davies 1991) the LEA can become an important advocate on behalf of and with parents and students. More generally one of the primary tasks of the new local government of education will be to promote public choice and accountability by presenting information, evaluating performance and, in particular, by enabling public discussion about achievement and educational purpose.

The achievements of local government in education have been considerable, indeed, 'there has never been a good idea that was not first tried and tested by a local education authority' (AMA). The list is impressive, including the under five service, community education together with the adult and youth services, support for bi-lingual learners and multi-cultural curriculum development as well as policies promoting equal opportunities. The range and quality of choice in further education, as Collier (1991) argues, reflects the essence of local government rather than the edicts of Whitehall or Moorfoot.

The local education authorities in this study exemplify this tradition of creative innovation in the reform of local education. They illustrate the conditions for the effective working of a reformed education service. Because education is a national public service each LEA has entered into the spirit of reform and is playing its part in the creation of a framework that is common throughout the land. Within a unitary democracy this is entirely as it should be. And yet there is significant local variation. Each LEA has brought a distinctive perspective to the management of change that derives from a consideration of local needs and demands. Upon local government lies the inescapable task of both reinterpreting national purpose to local need and generating the shared public purpose that is the precondition for local public confidence and commitment, so that the reforms are both given and chosen. Only a very sophisticated social institution could bring off this demanding task and four exemplar LEAs have gone a long way to realising these exacting demands of the public domain.

References and further reading

Audit Commission 1989 *Losing an Empire, Finding a Role: The LEA of the Future* Occasional Papers, No. 10 HMSO.

Bogdanor, V. 1991 'Where will the buck stop?' *Times Educational Supplement* 14 June.

Briault, E. and Smith, F. 1980 *Falling Rolls in Secondary Schools*, NSER.

Collier, A. 1991 'A sense of loss' *Times Educational Supplement* 19 April.

DES 1987 Press release, 20 November.

DES, 1988 *1988 Education Reform Act* HMSO.

DES, 1991 *Education and Training for the 21st Century*, HMSO.

DoE, 1988 *Local Government Act 1988*, HMSO.

Davies, H. 1991 'In search of a new role' *Times Educational Supplement* 15 March.

Davies, H. 1991 'Put people first' *Times Educational Supplement* 2 August.

Hargreaves, D. 1990 'Shedding a tier' *Times Educational Supplement* 9 November.

Maclure, S. 1988 *Education Re-formed* Hodder and Stoughton.

Maden, M. 1990 'Dangers in DIY democracy' *Times Educational Supplement* 30 November.

O'Connor, M. 1990 'Schools out' *New Statesman and Society* 14 December.

Peters, T. and Waterman, R. 1981 *In Search of Excellence* Harper and Row.

Ranson, S. 1989 'From 1944 to 1988: Education, citizenship and democracy' in Flude, M. and Hammer, M. (eds) *The Education Reform Act: Its Origins and Implications* Falmer.

Ranson, S. 1990 'Education' in Deakin, N. and Wright, A. (eds) *Consuming Public Services* Routledge.

Ranson, S. 1991a *The New Management of Education* A Report to the Local Government Management Board.

Ranson, S. 1991b 'Notes towards a dataset and a theory of local emergent systems of education', *BEMA's Annual Conference Paper*.

Ranson, S., Hinings, B. and Greenwood, R. 1980 'The structuring of organisational structures' *Administrative Science Quarterly* **25**, No 1.

Ranson, S. and Thomas, H. 1989 'Education reform: consumer democracy or social democracy?' in Stewart, J. and Stoker, G. (eds) *The Future of Local Government* Macmillan.

Rogers, M. 1991 *Three Years of Opting Out: An Analysis* Local Schools Information Unit.

Stewart, J. 1983 *Local Government: the Conditions of Local Choices* George Allen and Unwin.

Stewart, J. 1984 'Decentralisation and local government', Fabian Tract, 496.

Stewart, J. 1989 'A future for local authorities as community government' in Stewart, J. and Stoker, G. (eds) *The Future of Local Government*, Macmillan.

Stuart, N. 1989 Lecture to the 18th BEMAS Annual Conference.

SEO, 1991 *Roles and Responsibilities within the Nationally Maintained Education System* Society of Education Officers, London, June 1991.

Thompson, Q. and Parison, N. 1989 'Management of change in education' *Pubic Money and Management* **19** No. 1.